C000140151

Bible Plants and Animals

Volume 1

MAMMALS

Harry J. Baerg

REVIEW AND HERALD® PUBLISHING ASSOCIATION
WASHINGTON, DC 20039-0555
HAGERSTOWN, MD 21740

Copyright © 1989 by
Review and Herald® Publishing Association

The author assumes full responsibility for the accuracy of all
facts and quotations as cited in this book.

This book was
Edited by Gerald Wheeler
Cover design by Bill Kirstein
Cover lettering by Aaron Presler
Type set: 10 pt. Clearface Regular

Texts credited to NEB are from *The New English Bible*. © The Delegates of the Oxford University Press
and the Syndics of the Cambridge University Press 1961, 1970. Reprinted by permission.

Bible texts credited to RSV are from the Revised Standard Version of the Bible, copyrighted 1946, 1952
© 1971, 1973.

Texts credited to NIV are from the *Holy Bible, New International Version*. Copyright © 1973, 1978,
International Bible Society. Used by permission of Zondervan Bible Publishers.

PRINTED IN U.S.A.

R&H Cataloging Service

Baerg, Harry J.
    Bible plants and animals.
    3 v.

    Vol. 1, Mammals. Vol. 2, Birds
and other animals. Vol. 3, Plants.

    1. Bible—Natural History.   I. Title.
II. Title: Mammals. III. Title: Birds
and other animals. IV. Title: Plants.

      220.85

Library of Congress Cataloging in Publication Data

Baerg. Harry J.
    Bible plants and animals: natural history of the Bible / Harry J. Baerg.
      p.   cm.
    Contents: v. 1. Mammals
    1. Animals in the Bible—Dictionaries. 2. Plants in the Bible—Dictionaries.
3. Bible—Dictionaries. I. Title.
BS663.B34   1989
220.8'574—dc20   89-32937
                                  CIP

ISBN 0-8280-0498-6

Preface

This series of books is intended to provide reliable descriptions and illustrations of all the animals and plants mentioned directly or indirectly in the Scriptures. It does not pretend to be an exhaustive study of the meanings of the Hebrew or Greek terms used. I have listed what I consider to be the most reasonable linguistical and contextual choices of those suggested by the many Bible scholars and translators who have studied and written on the subject.

My primary thrust has been to give a realistic graphic and word picture of the animal or plant in question, to relate it to ones the reader may be familiar with, and to make the Bible story more real and vivid to the average modern reader.

The Bible is primarily the story of people and their relationship to their Creator. Though it makes a number of apt and discerning comments on certain creatures, it does not pretend to be a textbook on science. Bible authors, as well as the people for whom they wrote, often included several species or genera under a single name—they classed most small birds as sparrows and most small animals under the name of mice. The larger, more familiar living things usually received specific names, but not always. Animals such as the lion, bear, or wolf present no confusion, but with others we often find considerable disagreement in translation. I have taken the familiar King James Version as a basis to work from, but I have also used quite a number of more recent translations to shed light on names that are in doubt.

Transliteration Table:
Hebrew, Roman Script

Hebrew	Roman	Pronunciation
א	ʾ	the unwritten initiation of the first vowel in "able."
ב	b, *b*	b = b, as in *boy*; *b* = v, as in *weave*.
ג	g, *g*	g = g, as in *get*; *g* = g, as in German *Tag*.
ד	d, *d*	d = d, as in *door*; *d* = th, as in *the*.
ה	h	= h, as in *Harry*. Untransliterated when part of vowel.
ו	w	= w, as in *will*. Untransliterated when part of vowel.
ז	z	= z, as in *zero*.
ח	ḥ	= ch, as in Scottish *loch*; German *Buch*.
ט	ṭ	= emphatic t.
י	y	= y, as in *you*. Untransliterated when part of vowel.
כ, ך	k, *k*	k = k, as in *king*; *k* = ch, as in German *Buch*.
ל	l	= l, as in *love*.
מ, ם	m	= m, as in *madame*.
נ, ן	n	= n, as in *none*.
ס	s	= s, as in *sun*.
ע	ʿ	= emphatic laryngeal; no equivalent in European languages.
פ, ף	p, *p*	p = p, as in *pull*; *p* = ph, as in *phantom*.
צ, ץ	s	= emphatic s, like tz in *Blitzkreig*.
ק	q	= emphatic k.
ר	r	= r, as in *rub*.
שׂ, שׁ	ś, š	ś = s, as in *sin*; š = sh, as in *shin*.
ת	t, *t*	t = t, as in *tan*; *t* = th, as in *thin*.

There are no vowels in the Hebrew alphabet (*aleph, he, waw,* and *yod* are sometimes used to indicate vowels). Some Medieval Jewish scholars devised a system of marks, called "points," to indicate the traditional vowel sounds. These are transliterated below.

a = a, as in *father*.	i = i, as in *pin*.
ā or â = a, as in *all*.	î = i, as in *machine*.
e = e, as in *bed*.	ō, ô = o, as in *more*.
ē = e, as in *fiancé*.	u = u, as in *put*.
ê = ey, as in *they*.	û = u, as in *rude*.

In addition, there are very short, almost elided vowels called *shewas*. These are transliterated as follows:

ĕ = e, as in *characteristic*.

ă = a, as in *amount*.

ŏ = o, as in *obey*.

Style and abbreviations used in text:

NAME, COMMON; other names (Hebrew or Aramaic) (Greek); *scientific name.* H L W

Example:

DONKEY; Ass ('athon, chamar) (onos, hupozugion); *Equus asinus somalicus.* H 42″

Measurements:
H: approximate shoulder height in inches (″) or feet (′)
L: length of study skin, nose to hind toes in inches (″) or feet (′)
W: wingspread in inches (″) or feet (′)

Summer

Winter

ADDAX; pygarg (dishon); *Antelope nasomaculatus.* H 42″

The King James Version of the Bible translated the name of this animal as pygarg, meaning "white-rumped." *The New English Bible* calls it the white-rumped deer. Most authorities, however, are convinced that the addax is the animal really referred to. It is not a deer but an antelope that in Bible times ranged from the desert regions of northern Africa to include southern Palestine.

About the size of a donkey, both sexes of the addax have four-foot-long, spiraling, ribbed horns. In color it is a pale brownish gray that changes to reddish brown in winter. A white band across the face looks like a bandage. The legs, belly, and rump are also white. The name "white-rumped," seems to apply to it more than to any other Palestinian game animal. In winter it grows a clump of dark hair on its forehead and a long, black mane on the throat, but none on the back of the neck where we are used to seeing a mane.

The name addax appears only once in the Bible, in Deuteronomy 14:5 (as a clean animal, since it divides the hoof and chews its cud). Mounted hunters caught addaxes by driving them into nets or pits. The addax cannot run quite as fast as the swift gazelle, but it does well in the sandy

7

deserts where it lives, because its wide-spreading hooves help support its weight on the soft sand.

During the dry seasons it can go for long periods without drinking any water. It puts the camel to shame on that score. Apparently it manufactures water from the carbohydrates in its food or gets enough from the plants it eats. When rains do come to the desert, the addaxes see the thunderstorms from far off and head in that direction. They drink from the puddles and eat the green grass that flourishes in the wake of the moisture.

Canon Henry B. Tristram, a British Bible scholar who spent some time in Palestine making a study of the natural history of the Bible, saw an addax near the Dead Sea in 1863-1864. He stated that the Bedouins there knew the antelope, but it was by then quite rare. The last one in Palestine was killed in 1900. It is near extinction in the rest of its range now. Only a few small bands still roam remote areas of Algeria and the Sudan.

AOUDAD; Barbary sheep (zemer); *Ammotragus lervia.* H 36″

The one reference to it in the KJV, Deuteronomy 14:5, calls this animal the chamois, but that is most certainly a mistranslation, for the chamois is a wild goat of the Alps and has never lived in Palestine. The Hebrew word *zemer* means "leaper" and seems to indicate that it was agile and lived in a rocky habitat. The aoudad, (pronounced ah-oo-dad) is likely the animal meant here. It is a goatlike mountain sheep once common in Egypt and southern Palestine, but now wild only in the Atlas Mountains of northern Africa.

A large sheep, the aoudad stands three feet high at the shoulder, with wide-spreading, heavy horns that may grow to be more than two feet long. The creature lives in small flocks on high, rocky ground. Powerful and extremely agile, it leaps from rock to rock without losing its footing.

Long, dark hair on its lower neck and knees distinguish it from all other sheep. In color it is a uniform tan that matches the rocks on which it lives and makes it difficult to see when it is standing still.

The aoudad can go for days without drinking water, but when long-continued droughts kill the sparse vegetation in its inhospitable range in the dry mountains, the sheep also die off. They do well in captivity and live in a number of zoos around the world.

The mouflon, *Ovis musimon,* is another possible choice for the term *zemer*, though it is likely that the one name included both animals. This wild sheep now lives only in Corsica and Sardinia, though man has introduced some into the Balkans, and the animals are doing well there. In Bible times the mouflon also inhabited the mountains of Lebanon and other Mediterranean localities. Only the males have horns, enormous and ribbed like those of some goats and antelopes. Reddish-brown in color, the sheep has a whitish saddle-shaped mark over the back and sides in winter. It is smaller than the aoudad, only 27 inches high at the shoulder. Some biologists consider the mouflon to be one of the early ancestors of the domestic sheep. At times it will herd with domestic flocks in mountain pastures and become quite tame. Many game farms and zoos keep them, and they seem to do well in captivity.

APE—see Monkey

ASS—see Donkey

ASS, WILD—see Onager

European Bison

Aurochs

AUROCHS; wild ox, unicorn (re'em); *Bos primigenius*. H 6′

Under the heading "Unicorn" you will find a discussion of why older translators used that term for *re'em*, and why it should have been translated "aurochs" instead. This huge ancestor of our domestic cattle stood as much as six feet tall at the shoulder and measured 12 feet in length. It was indeed a powerful animal as described in Numbers 24:8, Deuteronomy 33:17, Job 39:9-12, Psalms 22:21 and 92:10, and Isaiah 34:7. Listen to the description given to us in Job 39:9-12: "Will the unicorn be willing to serve thee, or abide by thy crib? Canst thou bind the unicorn with his band in the furrow? Or will he harrow the valleys after thee? Wilt thou trust him, because his strength is great? or wilt thou leave thy labour to him? Wilt thou believe him, that he will bring home thy seed, and gather it into thy barn?"

God here describes to Job an animal that could do the work of an ox but is too powerful and wild for man to bring under his control. The depiction fits the character of the aurochs perfectly. Actually early man tamed and domesticated the aurochs, but that was probably done by capturing the calves.

The aurochs bull had long, forward pointing horns and a heavy neck. It was coal-black but had a white stripe down its back like a Hereford and

10

AUROCHS
1. Cave painting
2. Early drawing
3. On Ishtar Gate

white markings on its snout. The aurochs appeared in early bas-reliefs, and about A.D. 1500 someone, presumably an artist who had seen the creature, made a painting of one on wood. Cave paintings of them also exist. The present day gaur of Indonesia and the gayal of Burma give us some idea of what such early cattle looked like. The cows were smaller than the bulls, dark brown in color, and also had the white stripe down the back.

Thutmose III of Egypt enjoyed hunting aurochs, and on one expedition claimed to have killed 75 out of a herd of 176. Obviously he must have headed a large party of hunters. Small wonder that the animals became extinct. The Assyrian kings, on horseback, chased the aurochs. It may be for this reason that the remaining animals chose to live in the forests instead of the open country.

The wisent, or European bison, *Bison bonasus*, often is confused with the aurochs. The wisent was a smaller animal with a big hump on its shoulders, a shaggy mane, and short, curved horns like the American bison. It roamed the same extensive range as the aurochs and Bible writers were probably familiar with it as well. Quite possibly the term *re'em* applied to both wild cattle. European cave dwellers drew pictures of the wisent on their walls also.

The bison survived in eastern Europe and the Caucasus until shortly after World War I when the last member of a captive herd in Poland was shot. Scientists have attempted to breed back both the bison and the aurochs from domestic cattle. Their efforts have been quite successful.

BABOON—see Monkey

BADGER—see Ratel, also Dugong

BADGER, ROCK—see Hyrax

Mouse-eared Bat

Fruit Bat

BAT ('atalleph); *Chiroptera*. L 1″-16″ W 6″-72″

The Hebrew word for bat evidently included all the nearly twenty species today recorded in Palestine. Bats get mentioned as unclean "birds" in both Leviticus 11:19 and Deuteronomy 14:18. Though they are mammals, people in Bible times thought of them as birds because they could fly. Sometimes the ancients regarded them as a cross between birds and mammals, because though they could fly, they had fur instead of feathers.

To most people, bats are repulsive enough to make the command not to eat them unnecessary. Creatures of darkness, they live on insects and often have grotesque features. They have leathery wings with claws protruding from the edges. During the day they hang upside down, wings folded, packed together in large numbers in caves or attics year after year, until the accumulated droppings cause a stench in such unventilated areas. In addition, they are infested by hordes of parasites. As if this were not enough, absurd legends have grown up about them that associate them with the prince of darkness.

Fortunately the real bat is quite different. A harmless and quite beneficial creature that rids the environment of many insect pests, it has less connection with Satan than man has, and it strictly minds its own business.

The large fruit-eating bats, relatives of the "flying foxes" native to Asia, Africa, and Australia, have also been found in Bible lands. Attractive and clean, they hang from the branches of tall trees during the day and feed on fruit at night. A number of non-Jewish people eat them, and they could be ones the Levitical restriction has in mind.

BEAR, SYRIAN BROWN (dob) (arctos); *Ursus syriacus.* L 60″

The species of bear mentioned by the Bible writers is the Syrian brown bear, closely related to the giant Alaska species but not nearly as large. The Alaska brown bear can weigh up to 1,500 pounds, the Syrian only 300-500 pounds, not much more than a black bear. Next to the polar bear, it is the lightest colored of them all. Young Syrian bears are dark brown, but as they grow older they fade in color until nearly white.

Omnivorous, bears eat almost anything edible. Each spring they feed ravenously on the new vegetation, then vary their diet with ants and grubs that they find in rotten logs. They also catch young deer or lambs. During the fall they fatten up for winter on berries and spawning fish. In cold climates they hibernate in caves for winter. While in hibernation they give birth to their young—tiny, naked, and helpless creatures. By spring the newborn are furred and able to run about.

Bears usually hunt alone. About the only time when one sees more than one bear is during mating or when a mother is with her cubs. Ordinarily bears mind their own business and do not attack people, but when a mother thinks her cubs threatened, she will attack fiercely.

Bible writers noticed this. In 2 Samuel 17:8, Hushai, in trying to dissuade Absalom from following his father, David, who had fled, describes him "as a bear robbed of her whelps in the field." Proverbs 17:12 refers to the same trait when it states, "Let a bear robbed of her whelps meet a man." And in Hosea 13:8, "as a bear that is bereaved of her whelps."

Second Kings 2:24 records a bear story most of us have problems with. We want to explain away some of it to children. It appears that some young people made fun of Elisha after he had seen Elijah go up in a chariot of fire to heaven, calling him a baldhead. He cursed them, and two she bears came out of the woods and "tare forty and two children of them." Recent scholarship helps a little. "Youths" appears to be a better translation than "little children," and the bears mauled them instead of tearing them apart. If a gang of lawless teenagers threatened the prophet, we can understand his malediction a bit better. Likely it was a gang of 42, and the bears attacked the nearest ones and the rest ran away. The record does not say that the bears killed them all or that God commanded them to.

Bears were common in Palestine during Bible times. They lived in the forests and rocky canyons and were a nuisance to gardeners and shepherds as their relatives are today. David as a shepherd had to defend his flock against a bear that took a lamb (1 Sam. 17:34-37). Since then, bears have become more and more scarce, partly because of the disappearance of the forests, till during World War II soldiers shot the last ones for sport. A few Syrian bears still live in zoos. In Turkey and Persia a slightly different species continues to exist in the wild.

BEHEMOTH—see Hippopotamus

BOAR—see Swine

BOAR, WILD (chazir); *Sus scrofa*. H 36″

Wild boars inhabited the forests and marshes of Palestine during Bible times. Usually they stayed hidden during the day and came out at night, sometimes destroying vineyards, eating the grapes and pulling down the vines. A large herd could practically destroy a whole vineyard or garden in one night. No wonder the owners built watchtowers in their vineyards and walls around them. In Psalm 80:13 Asaph describes what sometimes happened, "The boar out of the wood doth waste it, and the wild beast of the field doth devour it." This is the only reference in the Scriptures that explicitly names the wild boar. In Psalm 68:30 of the New International Version of the Bible we read, "Rebuke the beasts among the reeds," and in *The New English Bible,* "those wild beasts of the reeds." This seems almost certainly to refer to the wild hogs.

In the reeds, their preferred habitat, the boars did little damage. But in the forests they rooted up much of the ground, destroying young seedlings and eventually the forests themselves. Feral razorbacks have caused extensive damage in the southern United States. It is quite obvious that when their numbers increase, rooting hogs can injure even mature forests.

The wild boar of Palestine was very similar to the European animal. A large male stood about three feet high at the shoulder, though the females were quite a bit smaller. Covered with coarse, dark brown to black hair, they had a stiff, bristly mane on the neck and down the back. The boars were quite different from the corn-fed porkers on our farms. Rangy and tough, they could run almost as fast as a horse and were adept at dodging. When cornered, they proved themselves fierce fighters. A boar with his sharp, upturned tusks could rip open a horse or disembowel a dog with lightning speed.

Wild boars are omnivorous, able to devour and digest nearly anything edible. In general, their diet consists of roots, tubers, mushrooms, fruit, snakes, mice, frogs, birds, carrion, and garbage. Both Jews and Muslims consider them unclean, but they still hunt them as pests and for trophies. They sell the carcasses at reasonable rates to Christians who might buy.

A litter often has as many as a dozen piglets. The young have markings of longitudinal stripes and spots. Young domestic piglets, though descended from the wild ones, do not have such camouflage patterns, but in young razorbacks that have gone wild for some time the pattern seems to appear again. Wild boars run in packs, called sounders, made up of extended family groupings.

Many different species of wild boars exist around the world. Africa has the giant wild boar, the red river hog, the wart hog, and others. In Asia, Indochina, and Indonesia porkers, both wild and tame, comprise an important food supply. They inhabit the most distant of the South Sea Islands. Palestine may still have a few living in the Jordan River marshes and on Mount Hermon, but they are no longer a threat to the farmers' crops.

BUBAL; hartebeest (yachmur); *Alcelaphus buselaphus.* H 40″

Called fallow deer in the KJV, this animal has been probably more correctly translated in the Septuagint as bubalos. The bubal is not a deer but an antelope, and it is closely related to the other hartebeests, the wildebeest, or gnu. The Arabs called it a wild cow, and it certainly looks more like that than an antelope. This particular species of hartebeest has an exceptionally long face, and some have thought of it as a horned horse.

The hartebeest is a rather timid animal that will usually sooner run than fight. It starts off in a rather stiff-legged gallop, but soon speeds up, then disappears in a cloud of dust. When cornered, it will fight fiercely with its short, back-curved horns. The animals sometimes feed with range cattle and become so used to man that they are soon tame and gentle, as if they had always been domestic. Solomon probably kept bubals in pens to serve as food on his table (1 Kings 4:23). The one other reference to it in the Bible is Deuteronomy 14:5, which classifies it as a clean animal that chews its cud and has cloven hooves.

This hartebeest ranges widely over much of northern Africa, and during Bible times it was quite common in Palestine. Even now it lives around the edges of the Sahara and up and down the Nile Valley. It feeds largely on grass. During the dry seasons it can go for long periods without water. Since both men and lions relish its flesh, it has reason to be watchful. Often one posts itself as a sentry on the top of a termite hill in the long grass country to warn of approaching danger.

Camel

Water Buffalo

BUFFALO, WATER ('aluph); *Bubalus bubalis*. H 60"

The water buffalo may not have lived in Palestine during Bible times, but it is common now in the low-lying Jordan Valley, and has been for hundreds of years. It is larger than other cattle and quite docile. For that reason it is useful as a draft animal, for operating water lifts for irrigation, and for turning grinding wheels. Farmers have introduced it from its native India and southern Asia into quite a number of tropical countries and islands.

A rather ugly animal, the water buffalo is usually clumsy, awkward-looking, and sleepy-eyed. To escape insect pests and the heat it will roll in mud or lie in shallow water for hours at a time with only its head exposed, placidly chewing its cud. Its horns may be exceptionally long and spread widely in a horizontal sweep. The Jews usually obeyed the biblical injunction against yoking an ox with an ass, but plowmen often hitch the buffalo and the camel to their crude plows in Arab lands.

BULL—see Cattle

BULL, WILD—see Oryx
BULLOCK—see Cattle
CALF—see Cattle

CAMEL, BACTRIAN (gamal); *Camelus bactrianus.* H 10′

The Bible does not specifically mention the Bactrian camel, but the Assyrians did use it, and the Israelites must have become acquainted with it during their captivity there. An obelisk erected at Nimrud (841 B.C.) shows two Bactrian camels as part of the booty of Shalmaneser III in northern Persia.

The two-humped camel often served as the beast of burden of the caravans used on the silk route from China, frequently hitched to carts drawn by means of a yoke that rested on their necks. The camels referred to in Isaiah 21:7 as hitched to a chariot may have been Bactrian. The Bactrian camels are slow and a bit clumsy, but they are sturdy and able to endure long journeys. Because they have a thick underfur and long coarse hair, they can endure the cold weather on mountain passes.

Some of the long hair provides the bristles for camel-hair watercolor brushes, some gets woven into a rough cloth for tenting material, and the soft underfur forms the basis of a fine cloth for expensive camel hair coats.

Bactrian and Arabian camels are not too distantly related, for they will

19

interbreed and have fertile offspring. Apparently some wild two-humped camels still exist, or did until quite recently, in the Lob Nor region of China.

CAMEL; Dromedary (gamal, bekar, rekesh, rammak, bikrah, achashteranim) (kamelos); *Camelus dromedarius.* H 10′

The camel appears rather smug, supercilious, and disdainful as he looks down from his lofty height. Apparently he hates to associate himself with any man or beast. Actually he seems to hate everything, even his own kind, and will kick, bite, or spit upon anyone in reach for little or no reason at all.

He seldom looks happy. It is said that he groans whenever someone puts a load on his back, no matter if it is only an orange, and that he protests every step as he plods along. His life seems to be one of unrelieved misery. Sir Francis Palgrave, who knew of camels from personal experience, said of him, "He is from first to last an undomesticated and savage animal, rendered serviceable by stupidity alone. . . . Never tame, though not wide awake enough to be exactly wild."

The camel's appearance gives him little to be smug about. He is awkward looking with big feet and splayed hind legs, knobby, calloused knees, and big bare patches in his lumpy fur. His big belly, high hump, and long neck do nothing to improve his appearance.

The animal is admittedly stupid. He goes in whatever direction his head happens to be pointed. If he strays away from the caravan or his home, he makes no effort to get back. The animal never gets out of the way for anyone in a crowded street, and has no misgivings about scraping off a rider under a low archway. While he has good ears, he often ignores his rider's commands. But if someone mistreats him, the camel remembers, and often takes revenge to the point of killing his master several days later.

Yet, having said all this, we have to admit that the patriarchs of Bible times highly valued the beast, and the nomadic tribes of the desert still do. He is extremely well suited to life in that harsh environment, and it was not just by chance that man enlisted him in his service as early as he did. Because no wild, one-humped camels still exist as possible ancestors of the domestic kind, we can only guess at what they might have been like. The present breeds of single-humped camels comprise the heavily built freight camels and the more slender riding ones, also called dromedaries.

Since the earliest times camels have carried precious trade goods or household equipment and families on long treks across miles of rough desert terrain.

The pack saddle of a caravan camel consists of a narrow bag about eight feet long filled with straw, doubled back on itself, and sewed together at the two ends to make a doughnut-shaped cushion. This cushion fits around the camel's hump. A wooden frame rests on it, with the load strapped to it on either side.

The camel's handlers make it kneel so that they can load it more easily. It carries about 400 to 600 pounds of goods. The camel knows just how much it can, or will, carry; and if overloaded, it will refuse to get up. Once under way, it plods along steadily at about three miles an hour. Draft camels also plow fields, turn grinding and irrigating wheels, and pull wagons. In Isaiah 21:7 it appears that the ancients even used them to draw chariots.

"Dromedary" in its narrower definition refers to the light, long-legged riding camels of which Thomas E. Lawrence had much to say in his book *The Seven Pillars of Wisdom*. The British Camel Corps in Egypt, as well as the French Foreign Legion in Algeria, rode them. Fast-riding camels can go nine to ten miles an hour and can cover in excess of 100 miles in a day. They are the animals their owners like to brag about. There is as much difference between them and the heavy freighters as there is between an American thoroughbred racehorse and a Clydesdale draft horse.

The riding saddle is a lightweight, leather covered wooden frame with a high back and a tall post in front. The rider can grasp the post to steady himself or wrap his legs around while riding. Women usually traveled in baskets (called furniture in Genesis 31:34) slung on either side of the hump. The camels wore richly ornamented halters with attached thongs for leading, but the rider guided them by tapping them on either side of the neck with a stick or the hand. A fancy collar often ornamented the camel's neck, and bells or pom-poms hung from both the halter and the saddle.

The camel rider mounts his steed while it is in the kneeling position. Then the fun begins. First the animal gets up on its front legs, throwing its passenger back. Then it rises on its hind legs, whipping him forward, then rocking the rider back and forth like a bucking horse.

If the rider still remains on his mount, he is in for some more acrobatics. A galloping horse touches the ground in rhythmic succession with each of its four feet, making for smooth riding. A camel, on the other hand, is a pacer. It moves the two legs on one side forward and then the two on the other side. This tends to produce motion that is not all forward. One who has tried it describes camel riding as like "sitting cross-legged on a piano stool on a two-wheeled cart driven at full speed diagonally across a plowed field." Such motion is enough to make anyone seasick. That may be one reason why folklore calls the camel "the ship of the desert." Some camels are smoother riding than others. Experts claim that experienced cameleers get so used to the motion that they can at times even catch catnaps.

The height of the rider on a camel seems precarious to a beginner, but it does have advantages. On a hot day he catches whatever cooling breeze there may be. He can also see above the distortion of the shimmering heat waves near the ground.

A properly treated dromedary that performs well becomes not only something to brag about, but almost an object of affection. Arab riders on their long, monotonous journeys will sing to their mounts as the Western cowboys do to theirs. It probably has a soothing effect, much as the cowboy's crooning is supposed to keep nervous cattle from being "spooked." Some of the songs are spontaneous; others, like the following, have a long tradition, but modified and added to until they became endless:

Dear to me as the sight of mine eyes, art thou, O my camel!
"Precious to me as the health of my life, art thou, O my camel!
and so on ad infinitum. The rider sings in a low, soft voice, and with the tinkling of camel bells and creaking of saddle leather, it has quite a hypnotic effect, helping to pass the monotonous miles.

The camel is well adapted to life in the desert. It can close its slit nostrils during a sandstorm to keep out flying sand. Heavy eyelashes and an inner membrane that winks across the eye, brushing out the sand, protect the eyes. The prominent, bony projections above the eyes help shield them from the bright sun. The ears have fur inside and out, and the long neck raises the head above the drifting sand.

Ordinarily a camel can go about three days without water, but during cool weather individuals have survived as much as seven days without drinking. Such an ability seems remarkable and has received much publicity, but several antelopes, like the addax and the oryx, can go for much longer periods without drinking. The camel stores water in one of its stomachs as well as in body tissues. When without water to drink, it draws on these resources, rather than taking fluid from the blood as humans do. It can also tolerate changes in body temperature by a few degrees, perspires little, and thus loses a minimum of water.

Normally a camel drinks about five to seven gallons a day, but it can, when extremely thirsty, guzzle down as many as 20. It was no small favor that Rebekah tendered when she not only offered Eliezer a drink from the well but said she would water his camels also (Gen. 24)—the stranger had 10 of them!

For food the camel will eat almost anything it can find. Some have said that it could survive on the shavings in a carpenter shop. With its split upper lip, protected by heavy calluses, it manipulates the thorny twigs of desert shrubs into its mouth, cuts them off with its powerful incisors, grinds them up with its molars, and swallows the mulch. Its stomach can evidently take a large amount of roughage. At times the camel will even eat its master's tent. The animal will remasticate what it eats later, as it chews its cud.

Deuteronomy 14:7 classifies the camel as unclean because, although it chews its cud, it does not divide the hoof. Arabs often butcher and eat young surplus animals if they need meat. The Jews could probably have gotten around the restriction had Scripture not specifically named the camel, because it is an even-toed mammal and one could class the two toes in front of the foot pad as hooves. True, the pad behind them is not entirely cleft, but the foot still has quite an obvious cleavage. The tough, flexible pad spreads and keeps the animal from sinking in soft sand and also adjusts to the unevenness of rocky ground.

The camel does not like to walk on soft sand and will groan as it does so. It does well on hard trails and smooth rocks. While it can ford streams and rivers, it is not a good swimmer because its bloated belly tends to capsize it. Camels hate slippery mud. Their splayed hind legs have a tendency to slip out from under them and leave the poor beasts sitting down hard on their rears.

The hump of the camel consists mostly of fatty tissues and serves as a reservoir on which the camel can draw when food grows scarce. A starved camel has a small, flabby hump, but one in good condition has a large, firm one. It may weigh as much as 80 pounds, and Arabs consider it a delicacy.

The camel served the nomadic desert dwellers of Bible lands for more than just transportation and draft. A story is told of a traveler, lost in the desert and dying of thirst, who came upon a camel that had been dead a few days. He cut it open, and with the water he found in its stomach, he slaked his thirst, survived, and managed to reach his destination. However, those who have opened up dead camels tend to doubt the tale. They say that the water in the stomach is green with bile and has a strong flavor. Also, the smell of a camel's stomach is so foul that it would be impossible to drink the water from it, especially after the camel had been dead several days, without throwing it up again. Of course some people, especially those dying from thirst, are less squeamish than others.

The dung of a camel largely consists of indigestible fibrous material, which, when dry, burns well. For that reason it is important to the desert traveler as fuel. People eagerly gather it in the fields and along trails for campfires and family cooking. While on a caravan they will sometimes attach a net to the camel's rear to catch the droppings so that nothing will be lost. Dung, mixed with clay and straw, serves as mortar in building.

A soft wool covers the camel in winter. Pulled or shorn in spring, it can be spun into cloth used for tents such as Abraham lived in, or coats such as John the Baptist wore (Matthew 3:4). Leather tanned from the hides of camels provided material for sandals, harnesses, saddles, thongs, and water bottles.

People drink camel milk and also make it into cheese. Part of the present that Jacob sent ahead to his brother Esau was a herd of 30 milch camels. Middle East travelers who have used camel milk say that it is so rich that it stays in lumps when used in their coffee.

After a gestation period of 11 months the cow camel gives birth to a calf. The youngster, though ungainly at first, still looks better than its parents. It has soft fur all over its body, and its call is a "baa," like that of a sheep. A caravan will stop briefly at the birth of a camel. Then someone lifts the young calf onto a saddlebag, and everybody moves on. After resting and nursing that night, the young animal is ready to continue the journey the next morning on its own legs. Most baby animals are playful, but young camels seem to have no idea of what play is. Life is all too serious to them.

They nurse for about a year and tag along after their mothers for another three. When they are 5 or 6 years old, they are ready for work.

Usually when the Bible mentions camels, it has large numbers of them in mind. We read in 1 Samuel 30:17 that 400 young men escaped on the animals. When Benhadad, king of Syria, was ill and wanted Hazeal to contact Elisha about his illness, he sent a present of 40 camelloads of goods as a present (2 Kings 8:9). In 1 Chronicles 5:18-21 we find that Israel had at that time 50,000 camels, but only 44,760 soldiers. Job had 3,000 camels at the beginning of his afflictions, and 6,000 after he recovered.

Most ancient cities had small gates cut into the large ones, or else beside them, to allow late-arriving travelers to enter without making it necessary to open the already closed and locked larger ones. Some have occasionally referred to them as the "eye of the needle." A camel could not get through one of the small gates unless he was stripped of his load and caused to kneel and shuffle through on his knees. Jesus may have used this as an illustration in Matthew 19:24, saying, "It is easier for a camel to go through the eye of a needle, than for a rich man to enter into the kingdom of God." He would have to leave all his property behind and go on his knees.

CATTLE; beeves, kine, oxen ('aluph, baqar, ben baqar, 'egel, 'eglah, 'eglath, 'eglath shelishiyah, meech, meri', mishneh, par, parah, shor, tor) (bous, damalis, tauros); *Bos taurus.* H 60″

The word *cattle* originally just meant property—chattel. But by common usage it has come to mean bovine livestock. The word "oxen" formerly conveyed the sense that "cattle" does now, but today it means only the adult, castrated males, also known as steers and bullocks. They were formerly important for draft as well as beef. "Cattle" now includes bulls (herd sires), cows (adult milking females), heifers (females before calving), and calves (young of either sex less than a year old).

Mankind domesticated cattle early in his history, according to both the archaeological and Biblical records. In Genesis 4:20 we read that Lamech's son, Jabal, was the father of "such as have cattle." Herdsmen derived most of their early cattle from the wild aurochs, *Bos primigenius*, that lived in the whole Mediterranean region and beyond. The Egyptians began raising the Indian Zebu cattle, also originally from a branch of the aurochs, even before the time of Abraham, so it is possible that he may have been familiar with them and even owned some. The smaller, later breeds, like the Brown Swiss and Jerseys, are believed to have come from the celtic ox, *Box taurus longifrons*.

Because they had cloven hooves and chewed the cud, cattle, of course, came under the classification of clean meat according to the Levitical laws. A cow, in common with other ruminants, has four stomachs. Because the coarse grass she feeds on does not digest easily, she needs all of them. She has no upper front teeth, just tough gums, and grazes by tearing off grass between her lower front teeth and the upper gums. Quickly she chews it enough with her big molars to compact and mix it with saliva so she can swallow it. Then it goes to the first stomach, where it accumulates until room opens up in the next compartment. The second stomach has its walls lined with cells like a big honeycomb. As this stomach works the food about, it collects in the cells as cuds, mouth-sized balls of grass.

When the cow lies down to rest, she coughs up the cuds one at a time, and thoroughly chews them. Then she reswallows them to the third stomach. Here they remain stored till a large enough batch has accumulated to start the final digestion in the fourth stomach and the intestines. It is really quite a complicated process.

Among the Hebrews the herdsman was an important individual. The patriarchs all had large herds of cattle, rather than gold or bank accounts, that indicated their wealth. The owner himself usually looked after his cattle until his sons were old enough to do so. They were the prime interest of the family, and the nomadic owners usually moved from place to place to find grazing for their herds.

Jacob, working for his uncle Laban, used various means, as related in

Genesis 30, to add to his own growing herd. Laban agreed to give him all the spotted animals born in the herd as his pay for overseeing them. Jacob, not satisfied to let nature take its course, placed peeled willow withes in front of the cattle as they came to streams to drink and mate. Modern genetics rejects the idea of any prenatal influence from the peeled withes, but his flocks increased in spite of the fact that his equally deceitful uncle changed his wages ten times (Gen. 31:41).

Oxen were the workhorses of the Hebrews, being hitched by means of a heavy wooden yoke resting on their necks to the tongue of a cart, plow, or drag. The Bible often mentions the yoke as a symbol of service. A yoke of oxen was a pair of them. When the Israelites only used one ox, it pulled awkwardly with a strap around its neck and the trace on one side.

Elisha, as mentioned in 1 Kings 19:19, was plowing with 12 yoke of oxen when Elijah came to choose him as his successor. There were 12 plows and 12 plowmen, of whom Elisha was one, and he was in charge. The plow that he used was a crude, iron-tipped, heavy stick. A long beam connected it with the yoke. Such a crude implement could work only when the soil was moist. The farmer guided the plow as well as the oxen and managed to scratch the surface of the field to a depth of only three or four inches. Thus it involved no great property loss of complicated and irreplaceable implements when Elisha, as recorded, killed the oxen and used the plows for firewood to sacrifice them.

The ancients drove the oxen with goads, long, stout sticks with an iron point on one end with which to prod the animals. A chisellike mounting on the other end could be used to scrape the accumulated dirt from the plowshare when necessary. The goad sometimes served as a spear in fighting. In Judges 3:31 we read that Shamgar, one of the judges of Israel, killed 600 Philistines with an ox goad and delivered his people. The Egyptians, however, drove their oxen with a whip of hippopotamus hide.

The Hebrews also used oxen to thresh their grain. The animals either trampled the sheaves on the threshing floor or hauled a rough drag over them. A yoke of oxen pulled the drag while the driver stood on it to provide extra weight. As it slid over the ripe grain it rubbed the kernels free from the hulls. The farmer threw the empty straw aside and winnowed the grain in the breeze to get rid of the smaller chaff. Oxen that worked on the threshing floor were not to be muzzled, according to Deuteronomy 25:4. They had liberty to take a mouthful of straw when they wished, because the laborer is worthy of his hire.

After threshing and sacking the grain, the farmer took it to storage or to market in a crude, two-wheeled cart drawn by oxen.

Cows also served as draft animals at times. In 1 Samuel 6 we read the story of how the Philistines returned the ark to Israel by means of cows yoked to a new wagon.

Genesis 41:2-4 describes Pharaoh's dream of the fat and the lean cattle appearing out of the river, and of the seven lean animals eating up the seven fat ones. Joseph interpreted it to mean that seven years of famine would follow seven years of bountiful harvests. He also suggested a storage plan whereby the ruler could profit by impending famine. It led to Joseph's appointment as prime minister in charge of the program.

The Egyptians worshiped a number of animals, including the black bull, Apis, which they even mummified. During their enslavement in Egypt the Israelites apparently learned to worship cattle. When God, through Moses, led them out of the country, His express purpose was to return them to the worship of the Creator only. Then, when Moses stayed too long on Mount Sinai, the people became impatient and persuaded Aaron to make a golden calf either for them to worship or to serve as a throne for the invisible Israelite God (Ex. 32:1-6). It greatly disappointed God that they should so soon return to the worship of the creature instead of the Creator.

About 500 years later Jeroboam set up two golden calves, one in Bethel and one in Dan, to serve as thrones for the invisible God of the universe. He wanted to keep the people of his kingdom from leaving Samaria to worship the Lord in the Temple at Jerusalem. His act lived on in infamy. Scripture mentions Jeroboam's name in connection with the phrase "which he made Israel sin" (1 Kings 15:30), referring to the incident recorded in 1 Kings 12:26-33.

God instituted various animal sacrifices to point His people to the sacrifice that Christ would eventually make, but it seems that the people soon lost sight of the real meaning of the rites and often appeared to perform the acts to earn salvation. Kings tried to outdo each other in the number of animals sacrificed. When Solomon sacrificed 22,000 oxen at the dedication of the Temple, it seems to us to have been an exceptionally extravagant waste of livestock. Actually it was not as extravagant as it sounds, for the priests burned only token parts of the animals. The rest of the carcasses went as food for the thousands of people who had gathered for the dedication.

Cattle had a number of additional uses. Their hides provided a source of leather for harnesses, saddles, and armor. Raw bullhide stretched over shields and dried hard became a light substance difficult to pierce with a spear or sword. The thongs and bag of David's sling likely consisted of cowhide. The ancient Israelites made moneybags from calf leather, and they used wet rawhide thongs to wrap the parts of their plows and wagons together. When the thongs dried and shrank, they tightened and made a solid joint.

Cows produced more milk than did sheep or goats. People used it fresh and also made it into cheeses. In Proverbs 30:33 we read, "Surely the churning of milk bringeth forth butter." We think of the golden butter on our tables made by churning cream in a sanitary churn, but the process, at that time was quite different. Milk, kept in unwashed goatskins, soured quickly. To hasten the process the farmer would shake or churn the bag. The soured milk clabbered and turned into curds that, when strained, pressed, and salted, made a kind of cream cheese called butter. In 1 Samuel 17:17, 18 we find that just before the Goliath incident young David came to the army with some loaves of bread for his brothers and some cheese for their captain. In 2 Samuel 17:29 we also read that Barzillai brought David and his men "cheese of kine" in the wilderness when he fled from Absalom. The cheese consisted of milk curds.

It is interesting to note that God made some regulations regarding the treatment of cattle. Exodus 23:4 and Deuteronomy 22:1 told the Israelites to return their neighbor's ox or ass if it strayed. In Exodus 20:10 the fourth commandment extends the Sabbath rest to cattle as well as to masters and servants. Deuteronomy 22:4 enjoins the Hebrews to assist a fallen ox or ass at the roadside. The restriction in verse 10, "Thou shalt not plow with an ox and an ass together," also seems to be of a humanitarian nature. However, the practice is still done, even in recent times, in many Middle Eastern countries.

CHAMOIS—see Aoudad

CONEY—see Hyrax

COW—see Cattle

DEER, FALLOW; *Dama dama.* H 40″

DEER, RED ('ayyal, ayyala, sebi, ya'alah); *Cervus elaphus.* H 54″

ROEBUCK (tsebi, sebeyah); *Capreolus capreolus.* H 30″

"As the hart panteth after the water brooks,
so panteth my soul after thee, O God" (Psalm 42:1).

At least three species of deer frequented Palestine in the days when forests still covered the mountains. One was the red deer, similar to that found in Europe. A large deer, it resembles the elk or wapiti of our western mountains. The second, the fallow deer, also lives in Europe. Smaller in size, it ranges in color from white to dark brown, but is usually tan, spotted with white in summer. It has palmate antlers.

The roebuck is a third Eurasian deer that was also common in Bible lands. We cannot, however, be sure that any scriptural passage specifically refers to it, even though the KJV employs the name. The roebuck is a small, secretive deer that comes out only at night. The bucks have short, upright spikes or forked antlers. Bones of reindeer and European elk (like our moose) have turned up in caves in Lebanon. It is unlikely that the Israelites would have classified them as deer.

The KJV calls the stag, buck, or male deer, by the archaic "hart." The doe, or female deer, goes by the name of "hind." The writer of 1 Kings 4:23

refers to "harts, and roebucks, and fallowdeer" being served at the king's table. The passage contains two mistranslations. The Hebrew *tsebi* should have been "bubal" instead of "fallowdeer." For additional information, see under those headings.

The meat of deer, classed as clean, appeared on Solomon's table. Isaac asked Esau to bring him savory venison before he bestowed on him the blessing of the firstborn. Venison is deer meat, but in this case scholars tend to think that the patriarch had in mind the flesh of the wild goat, the ibex.

In most of the deer family only the males have antlers, caribou and reindeer being exceptions. On most horned animals the horn is a hollow sheath that grows around a bony core that projects from the skull. Such horns are permanent, growing as long as the animal lives. The only ungulate that sheds its horns is the pronghorn antelope of the American west. Its horns have a bony core, and the outer shell sheds annually.

On deer the antlers, as they are called rather than horns, are solid. When the deer shed their antlers in late winter or early spring, they come off right at the skull. During the summer the bucks grow new antlers that will be ready for use in the fall. Usually they will grow a little larger than the year before, with additional points. Even the enormous racks of the caribou and the six-foot spread of the Alaska moose develop in one short season and then drop off again.

When Jacob blessed his 12 sons (Genesis 49:21), he said that Naphtali "is a hind let loose," suggesting that he was nimble as a deer. In Isaiah 35:6 we read, "Then shall the lame man leap as an hart," indicating how the infirmities and sicknesses of the present life will vanish in the earth made new. When forests still covered the Holy Land, the woods contained many deer. As David hid from Saul in the wilderness he must have seen the thirsty stags come down to the streams to drink in the evenings. The scene struck him as a fit and poetic simile to describe his great longing for the water of life that comes from God alone.

DOG (keleb) (kunarion); *Canis familiaris*. H 20″

"Yet the dogs eat of the crumbs which fall from the masters' table (Matt. 15:27).

Though loved and highly regarded in most of the world, the dog received only rejection from the Hebrews during Bible times. The Egyptians appreciated dogs, made statues of them, and even developed breeds of hunting dogs such as the greyhound and the saluki, but the Israelites did no more than tolerate them. Dogs must have accompanied them out of Egypt, and it is quite possible that the Israelites had ones of their own before that. Most likely they used them to help guard and drive their livestock, but they apparently never developed any real appreciation or affection for them.

People domesticated dogs from the original stocks of wolves and jackals early in human history. The remains of dogs have turned up in some of the lowest layers of the excavations of Jericho. Dogs also lived in Mesopotamia during Abraham's time. Today more than 400 different varieties exist in the world, though biologists consider all of them to be of one species. In most countries we find many different breeds of dogs, such as spaniels, collies, Saint Bernards, and others that breeders have developed from the original domesticated animals. But ancient Palestine had only one breed.

It was a short-haired, tan-colored, scrawny, slinking, savage beast, marked with the scars of a dozen fights. While it chose to live near man, it had no master. Ordinarily it had to find its own food or starve. The animal lived in any shelter it could find within its territory. Palestinian dogs divided up each town and city into districts claimed by family clans. Like the youth gangs of New York or Los Angeles, each clan had its own turf. No other dogs dared cross the invisible lines that marked its boundaries. Only when they attached themselves to a man who was crossing through did they dare to enter another clan's territory. When they did so, they stayed close to the man, and all the other dogs along the way snarled at them.

Tough and vicious though these dogs seemed to be, they had a better side to their natures. When shown kindness and provided food, they were known to give loyal, devoted service, guarding their benefactor and his property against all others of their kind.

The Bible mentions the dog numerous times, invariably as a creature despised and loathed. The most offensive thing that one could say of a man was to compare him to a dead dog. When Saul pursued David in the wilderness (1 Sam. 24:14), David shouted to him from a hilltop, "After whom is the king of Israel come out? after a dead dog, after a flea." After becoming king, he summoned Mephibosheth, Jonathan's son, to him. The crippled man protested in humility, "What is thy servant, that thou shouldest look upon such a dead dog as I am?" (2 Sam. 9:8). Later still, as David fled from Absalom (2 Sam. 16:9), Shemei cursed and reviled the refugee king—an act that was too much for the loyal Abishai. To David he exclaimed, "Why should this dead dog curse my lord the king?" He wanted to kill the man, but the king restrained him.

When Gideon chose his band of 300 men at the stream, God told him to reject the ones that lapped up water "as a dog" (Judges 7:5). Apparently the Philistines also had a low opinion of dogs. As David approached Goliath with his staff and sling the giant protested, "Am I a dog, that thou comest to me with staves?" (1 Sam. 17:43).

One of the worst things that could happen to a man when he died was for dogs to eat him; this was always a real threat in those days, for many of the destitute died in the streets. Criminals or those who had displeased rulers were also left to die there or thrown on the garbage heap after being beheaded. Many were buried in shallow graves in the "potter's field" where starving dogs could dig up the bodies and devour them. Only the rich could afford caves hewn out of the rock where they could place their dead safely behind a heavy rock door that had to be rolled away, as at the tomb where Joseph of Arimathea buried Christ.

For that reason it must have been quite a shock to Jeroboam when the prophet Ahijah predicted that his kingdom would later come to naught and that "him that dieth of Jeroboam in the city shall the dogs eat" (1 Kings 14:11). Elijah later renewed the prediction to Ahab after he had taken Naboth's vineyard (1 Kings 21:19).

Ahab died in battle, and his bodyguards took him to Samaria for burial, but as servants washed his chariot (1 Kings 22:38), the dogs licked his blood off it. Jezebel, his wife, the instigator of much of his wickedness, met an even worse fate (2 Kings 9:10, 30-37). On Jehu's command several palace eunuchs threw her out of the window to the street. Then, when Jehu came out to take care of her burial, the dogs had eaten all but her skull, hands, and feet.

In Psalm 22, from which Christ apparently quoted while on the cross, David says in verse 16, "For dogs have compassed me, the assembly of the wicked have enclosed me: they pierced my hands and my feet."

The New Testament, too, contains only derogatory statements about dogs. "Give not that which is holy unto the dogs" (Matt. 7:6). "It is not meet to take the children's bread, and cast it to the dogs" (Matt. 15:26). Christ Himself made both statements. "For without are dogs, and sorcerers, and whoremongers, and murderers, and idolaters, and whosoever loveth and maketh a lie" (Rev. 22:15).

We can find no apparent theological reason that the Scripture writers should despise dogs. It is more likely a cultural prejudice that colors the expressions of the people of that time and place. A similar antipathy affects some of the statements about women because of their place in that particular society. God accepted people where they were and tried to bring them slowly up to a higher understanding of the sanctity and dignity of all life.

DONKEY; ass ('athon, chamar) (onus, hupozugion); *Equus asinus* somalicus. H 42"

The donkey—or ass, as the Bible usually calls it—was one of the earliest domesticated animals. Both Abraham and Job had large numbers of them. Its supposed origin was the Somali wild ass, an animal of northern Africa now nearly extinct in the wild. This wild ass of Africa was typically gray with a white muzzle, eye patch, and underparts. The animal had black-tipped ears, black mane and tail, a black stripe down its back, and another across its shoulders. (The cross pattern intrigues the superstitious, for Christ rode an ass before His crucifixion.) It has narrow hooves and unusually large ears, and its call is a bray—all characteristics of the domestic donkey, but not of the other wild asses of Asia such as the onager and the kiang, which also enter the biblical writings. Africa also contains the Nubian, Algerian, Sudanese, and Red Sea wild asses that are quite similar to the Somali variety. Possibly the domestic breed's ancestry also stems from some or all of them. The domestic animal comes in several other colors as well, including black, brown, and albino. The Bible refers to the donkeys also as he-asses and she-asses, colts and foals. Americans usually speak of them as burros, jackasses, and jennies.

Donkeys were the poor man's horse in a sense, yet no stigma was attached to a man of higher position who used one. Balaam, as recorded in Numbers 22:21-35, traveled on one and had a unique conversation with it on his way to curse Israel. Governors and rulers had white asses as mounts (Judges 5:9, 10). Women and children often rode them. The wealthy Shunammite woman (2 Kings 4:24) took an ass when she went to get Elisha after her son had died. Jesus Himself rode an ass on His triumphal entry into Jerusalem. The gospels saw it as the fulfillment of the prophecy in Zechariah 9:9: "Thy King cometh unto thee: . . . lowly, and riding upon an ass, and upon a colt the foal of an ass." It appears to have been a gesture of humility, since he could as well have ridden a horse, but to the people of that time the horse was a symbol of war, and Christ was the Prince of Peace.

The rider did not control his mount by a bit in its mouth, but by a muzzle bridle. *It had a wide strap across the muzzle held in place by another over the head behind the ears. Reins attached to it enabled the rider to pull the head to the right or left. Proverbs 26:3 comments, "A whip for the horse, a bridle for the ass." People evidently considered the ass to be more manageable than the horse.*

The saddle usually consisted of a folded blanket with a straw bag on it and a colorful blanket or rug on top of that, all cinched around the donkey's belly with a thong. The Arabs seem to prefer sitting on the rear end of the animals, but most others like a position near the middle. The donkey has an easy gait, making it comfortable to ride. Some donkeys are deliberate in their movements; others walk more sprightly. On the whole, Scripture and the Middle East highly regard the little creature. An intelligent animal, it is surefooted and able to endure rough going. Fairly fast, the donkey can keep up with camels during long trips. On rough ground it can even keep ahead of horses. The usual picture we have of the donkey shows him stumbling along with his head down, but a well-treated animal holds his head high, steps lively, and can even canter or gallop when the occasion demands.

People in Bible times often used donkeys as bearers of burdens. They hung bundles of wood or grain on each side to give the animal a balanced load. Poles or planks tied on both sides trailed behind like an Indian's travois. Jacob said of one of his sons in Genesis 49:14, "Issachar is a strong ass, couching down between two burdens." The donkey sometimes had a load too big for it to bear, and it would collapse on the trail. Moses reminded the people (Ex. 23:5) that if they should see the ass even of one that hated them in such a predicament, they should surely help him. The ass was a bit small for plowing, but people in the Middle East have often disregarded the injunction in Deuteronomy 22:10: "Thou shalt not plow with an ox and an ass together."

Donkeys also widely served as motive power for turning grinding wheels, grape-crushing wheels, or lifting wheels for raising irrigation water from rivers into ditches. Blindfolded, they walked patiently in a circle all day long, pulling the attached pole and being kept in place by a tether line tied to the center. Sometimes the attendant would even attach a whip so that it would lift mechanically and fall on the donkey's rear end on every round to keep him moving.

If a donkey should stray away, he is in no danger of starving to death. He can live on thorns and thistles and other rough fare, and if any water is available, he will find it. Saul was out looking for his father's asses when Samuel met him and anointed him king. When he arrived home, he found that the asses had gotten there even before he did, proving that "the ass [knoweth] his master's crib" (Isa. 1:3).

Many feral burros, apparently descended from ones that strayed from prospectors, roam the Southwestern deserts. The animals live and prosper in their adopted home much as do the wild asses of the Old World. They also value their freedom in the same way, are alert to danger, and hold their heads high. When caught, they will struggle and fight, but when bridled with a load strapped to their backs, they plod along as though they have done it all their lives.

The various references to the ass in the Bible are generally complimentary. Even the comments of Balaam's ass, when the prophet struck it, sound more sensible than its master. It seems that in Bible times even dead asses had 101 or so uses. During the famine in the besieged city of Samaria (2 Kings 6:25), an ass's head sold for 80 pieces of silver. The most dramatic use, however, was that by Samson when he slew a thousand Philistines with the jawbone of an ass (Judges 15:15).

DORMOUSE—see Mouse

DUGONG; sea cow (tachash); *Halicore dugong.* L 9'

When the Israelites began to construct the tabernacle in the Sinai wilderness, God told them to use *tachash* skins for the outer covering of the roof. The KJV translates the word as "badgers" skins. *The New English Bible* renders it in Exodus 25:5 as "porpoise" with a footnote, "*strictly* sea cow." The American Standard Version says "sealskins," with "porpoise-skins" in the margin. Both porpoises and seals live in the nearby Red Sea. It is possible that the Israelites may have been able to get the skins of some of them for covering the tabernacle. The children of Israel were, however, not a seagoing people but herdsmen. Thus it is unlikely that they would have captured enough of the animals to cover the 500-plus square feet of the roof of the tabernacle.

But there is another possibility. The dugong, or sea cow, also a marine mammal, was common in the Red Sea and the Gulf of Aqaba, areas not far from the Sinai Desert. It feeds along the margins of inlets and tributaries, staying close to the shore and grazing on the algae, water hyacinths, sea grass, and other marine vegetation. Dugongs are gregarious, often feeding in herds of 10 to 20. The Hebrews could have cornered and killed quite a number of the sluggish, defenseless animals with spears and harpoons. Their hide is tough, and after tanning, it would have made a good covering for both the tabernacle and the furniture in it. The Israelites could also have used it for shoe soles as mentioned in Ezekiel 16:10. Bedouins in the desert near the sea still commonly employ it for that purpose.

Dugongs are 8 to 12 feet long and their hides are large enough to have been an appropriate covering for the tabernacle, much as the buffalo skins that plains Indians in our country employed for their tepees. The fact that the other items in the list containing the tachash were precious does not mean that this item could not be of a practical nature.

The dugong inhabits many of the coastal waters of eastern Africa, southeastern Asia, and Australia. In Florida, the Caribbean, and the tropical coast of western Africa we find a close relative of the dugong known as the manatee. It is quite similar in appearance to the above, but its flat tail is rounded at the end instead of notched like that of a whale.

ELEPHANT, AFRICAN, Ivory (habbim, shenhabbim, shen) (elephantica); *Loxodonta africana.* H 10′

ELEPHANT, ASIATIC; *Elaphas maximus.* H 8′

The Bible does not mention the elephant itself, but it does refer to the ivory of elephant tusks a number of times. Solomon had a throne of ivory so magnificent that it impressed the Queen of Sheba. Ahab, king of Israel, had an "ivory house" (meaning decorated with ivory). Archaeologists have unearthed what may be many of its decorations. Egyptian excavations reveal many artifacts of ivory, and so do those of Assyria and Babylon.

The ivory that Solomon and the Egyptians used came mostly from Ethiopia and Somaliland, via the Red Sea and the Nile River. That employed in Samaria and Assyria had its origin in Asiatic elephants. According to archaeological records, elephants ranged as far north as Syria and Mesopotamia during Bible times, and they served as royal game for kings. Thutmose III of Egypt, Tiglathpileser I, and Adad-nirari II of Assyria all bragged of hunting them.

The African elephant is a little larger than the Asiatic, has much bigger ears, heavier tusks, and two "fingers" on the end of its trunk instead of one. On the Asiatic elephant the tusks grow only on the males. The latter species more easily domesticates and will work in lumbering and other occupations. Most of the elephants in zoos and circuses are Asiatic.

The elephant is remarkable not only as the largest land mammal on earth (the African elephant can stand 11 feet tall and weigh more than six tons), but also because of its unique trunk. It is an elongation of its nose; the animal breathes and smells through it. It also uses the trunk to browse, picking off vegetation and stuffing the leaves and other plant material into its mouth. A typical elephant eats about 300 pounds of hay or forage in a day. The trunk is so versatile that an elephant can pick up a peanut from the floor or lift a teak log weighing 600 pounds. It draws up water with its trunk, then squirts it into its mouth and swallows it, drinking about 50 gallons a day. During hot weather it may squirt the water over its back to cool off. In addition, an elephant employs its trunk to feel or caress its young or another elephant.

In Bible times elephants served as engines of war (see 1 Maccabees 1:17; 6:30-46; 8:6; 11:56; 2 Maccabees 13:2-15). Studying the records and making allowances for obvious exaggerations and inaccuracies, we still get a fairly good picture of how armies used them. Antiochus Eupator led a huge army against Jerusalem that included 32 elephants. Partially armored, they had a wooden tower and panniers chained on their backs that contained armed soldiers. A mahout, who guided the elephant, sat on its neck. The elephants' handlers gave them wine or rice liquor before battle to put them in a fighting mood. Thus fortified, they charged, trumpeting, into the opposing ranks of soldiers, opening the way for cavalry, chariots, and foot soldiers to follow them. Modern war employs tanks in a similar manner.

Elephants were useful in battle for a while. Hannibal, the Carthaginian general, even led his army, including some elephants, over the Pyrenees and Alps into Italy during the Second Punic War. Much of the success of war elephants resulted from the element of surprise and terror invoked by seeing the furious monsters charging.

Soon military leaders counterattacked. In the Maccabean conflict Eleazar, son of Mattathias, dodging under the largest elephant, thrust his sword into its belly and died as it fell on him. Others soon learned that the animals' trunks were quite sensitive, so soldiers attempted to cut them with sharp swords and spears. The infuriated animals would turn and charge through the midst of their own forces. Other times the soldiers would open their ranks, allow the elephant to enter, then attack it from all sides till it died. The elephant soon became too unreliable to be much of an asset in battle.

Some have thought that the elephant was the animal referred to in Job 40:15-24 as behemoth. More authorities now agree that it is the hippopotamus, and we have listed the reasons for thinking so under that name.

EWE—see Sheep

FALLOW DEER—see Bubal

FENNEC—see Fox

FERRET—see Weasel

Red Fox

Fennec

FOX, RED (shual) (alopex); *Vulpes flavescent*. L 30″ See also Jackal.

FOX, DESERT; *Vulpes nilotica*.

FOX, EGYPTIAN; *Vulpes aegyptiaca.*
FOX, FENNEC; *Fennecus zerda.*

"Take us the foxes, the little foxes, that spoil the vines" (S. of Sol. 2:15).

In the Scriptures the Hebrew term *shual* and the Greek *alopex* evidently denote both the fox and the jackal. Most of the references deal with the jackal, and we will consider them later under that heading. Some could refer to both, and others definitely have the fox in mind.

Foxes range widely throughout the world, and at least four species in two genera have lived in countries where the Israelites sojourned. The ordinary European red fox dwelt in the northern part of Palestine, the desert fox in the southern deserts, and the Egyptian fox in Egypt. The latter two are lighter in color than the red, but otherwise quite similar. In their wanderings through the Sinai deserts the Israelites could also have come in contact with the fennec. This little fox weighs only two to three and one half pounds, but has ears up to six inches long. With such large ears, like radar antenna, it can detect the faintest sounds made by insects boring in the sand. Fennecs eat small rodents, reptiles, insects, and fruit. They could have been the "little foxes, that spoil the vines" referred to in the Song of Songs.

Unlike most other fox species, the ordinary red fox has a characteristic white tail tip and orange-colored fur. Most other kinds have a black or gray tail tip. The red fox now roams Australia, New Zealand, and North America because British sportsmen dearly loved their fox hunting and could not be without it. The fox has also crossed over into Alaska from Siberia and the two imports have spread till by now they range over most of North America. The red fox is not always red. The same litter may also have black, silver, or cross (a light buffy gray with a darker cross over the shoulders) pups.

The fox has received a special reputation for its craftiness, both in catching its prey and in escaping its pursuers. It will often double back on its tracks, jump aside and go in a different direction, wade creeks to destroy its scent, or otherwise confuse dogs and hunters on its trail. When told that Herod was looking for him (Luke 13:32), Christ referred to him as a fox, meaning that he was crafty.

Foxes hunt alone most of the time. Only in the mating season or when the mother is with her young do we see more than one at a time. They stay out in the open in summer and winter and sleep curled up with their sensitive noses hidden in their bushy tails. When the vixen is about to bear young, however, she digs a den in a wooded area or renovates an old one of another animal. Safe underground, she gives birth to three to twelve helpless young that she will nurse and feed till they are old enough to come out and learn to hunt with her. Jesus noted the fact that "the foxes have holes, and the birds of the air have nests; but the Son of Man hath not where to lay his head" (Matt. 8:20).

Lamentations 5:18 and Ezekiel 13:4 may be alluding to either a jackal or a fox. Both passages portray an inconsequential creature that appears and vanishes and does not leave a noticeable impression.

When Nehemiah's enemies ridiculed his work in rebuilding the walls of Jerusalem, they said, "if a fox go up, he shall even break down their stone wall" (Neh. 4:3). Even the light step of a fox could knock it down.

The red fox does love grapes and could easily be the one referred to in our introductory text from the Song of Solomon as "the little foxes." They were smaller than the jackals that some might have regarded as the big foxes. The still smaller desert fox might be a still more likely choice. The fennec, smallest of them all, could also have been the one, though it is less likely to visit settled grape-growing areas.

In Aesop's fables, written about the time of Daniel, we have the story of the fox that, unable to get some grapes hanging just out of his reach, decided that they were sour anyway. From it comes the phrase "sour grapes."

GAZELLE, DORCAS (tsebi, sebi, sebiyah) (dorcas); *Gazelle dorcas.* H 24″

The KJV uses "roebuck" in Deuteronomy 14:5 and other places for the Hebrew word *tsebi,* but gazelle is now the preferred translation. The gazelle, listed as a clean animal, was obviously regarded as a superior and tasty meat. Scripture mentions it as included in the food supplied for Solomon's table (1 Kings 4:23).

Of the 12 species of gazelle known in the Old World, three formerly lived in Palestine. Some still do. The three are quite similar in appearance and habits. The general color of the animals is a light brown with dark flank and shank stripes, a white belly and rear. The dark and white markings help to break up the color pattern and make the animals hard to spot in the shimmering heat waves of the deserts, where they prefer to live. Their eyes are large and beautiful.

Gazelles are exceptionally fast runners, some being clocked at 60 miles per hour. References in 2 Samuel 2:18 and 1 Chronicles 12:8 take note of their running ability. During Bible times men, riding in relays on the backs of fast horses, hunted them. Hunters also caught them in nets and pitfalls. When threatened by wolves, the adults in a band form a circle, horns outward, with the young in the center. Such behavior is, of course, no defense against high-powered rifles. Flight is better.

In the year 1900 gazelles were still quite plentiful in Palestine. Reports mention them in Galilee, Mount Carmel, and even on the Mount of Olives. Since then, hunting has nearly driven them to extinction. Today, under protection, they have multiplied again. One appeared recently on the Plain of Esdraelon in the same field as a farmer driving a tractor. Both Jordan and Israel have established them in sanctuaries, where their numbers have increased.

GERBIL—see Mouse

GOAT, ANGORA; *Capra angorensis.* H 30″
GOAT, COMMON; *Capra hircus.* H 30″
GOAT, NUBIAN ('allud, 'attud, ben 'ez, 'ez, gediyah, sa'ir, saphir, seirah, sephir, tayish) (eriphion, eriphos, tragos); *Capra mambrica.* H 28″

The goat was important to the Hebrews in Bible times. Sheep grazed in large flocks in the grassy valleys and open hillsides, but goats could manage in rocky, brush-covered slopes and canyons where sheep would get lost and starve. While sheep dependently followed the shepherd along the trails to the pastures, goats scrambled around over the steep, rough cliffs alongside. The latter needed no shepherd to protect them, but were wary and well able to look after themselves. Rocky high places challenged them.

At night when the shepherd guided his flock to the safety of the fold, the goats bounded down the rocky trails from the hillsides and leaped over the sheep to get into the fold. Once there, they preferred not to mix with the sheep, making it easy for the shepherd to separate the sheep from the goats when he needed to.

Sheep like to follow a leader, and without a shepherd they will often follow a horned billy goat who knows where he is going. In a large flock of sheep a scattering of goats helps to keep the sheep from bunching together too much and makes better grazing for all.

When abandoned on rocky islands, goats tend to multiply rapidly and overgraze, stripping the leaves and bark from trees and shrubs and devouring seedlings. Soon they will have left nothing but bare rocks.

Most of us are familiar with the European breeds of goats such as the Toggenburg and the white Saanen, but it is likely that the most common goat in the Holy Land was the Nubian. Usually black, it also comes in variations of brown with white blotches. It is a flop-eared breed with a big Roman nose, usually short-haired, and well adapted to hot climates. To get at the leaves, it will climb trees, and thorns do not seem to bother it. The people of Palestine also raised the Angora goat of Persia. It had a long coat of curly ringlets of mohair that one can weave into cloth.

The flesh of the adult male goat is usually tough and stringy, and has a strong odor. For this reason people do not usually eat it. Does are needed for milk and to produce kids, but the young males are tasty and can be killed and eaten. They are a delicacy for the table. Rebekah prepared two kids for her husband, Isaac, when he requested venison from Esau, helping to deceive him into giving Jacob the birthright instead of Esau (Genesis 27). Gideon and Manoah both prepared a kid for the angels who came to visit them (Judges 6:19 and 13:15).

The goat was the poor man's cow, and the kid was the animal of least value that one could kill for a feast. The older brother of the prodigal son complained to his father that he had not even received a kid to feast on with his friends, but for his brother, who had wasted his father's substance, the father slew the fatted calf (Luke 15:29, 30).

Goats produce more milk than sheep do. It is less rich, but more easily digested than that of either sheep or cows. In Middle Eastern countries cooks sometimes prepared meat by boiling it in milk in its last stages. God told the Israelites in Exodus 23:19, "Thou shalt not seethe a kid in his mother's milk." The prohibition did not condemn their culinary custom, but was apparently aimed at a fertility rite among the Canaanites that God did not want His people to follow.

The Israelites spun and wove the hair of ordinary goats into coarse clothing and tenting, but cloth made from the long, soft mohair of the Angora goats is a much finer fabric. It was classed with the precious items collected for the building of the tabernacle in the wilderness (Ex. 25:4). The Hebrews also used goat hair for stuffing pillows. In 1 Samuel 19:13 we read the story of Saul's daughter placing an image in David's bed on a goat-hair pillow and covering it up to make it appear that David was sick in bed. As a result she saved him from her father's wrath.

Leather made from goatskins is of a fine quality. Stronger than that of sheep, it does not scuff as easily. The skins of young goats had the hair removed and were stretched to make the fine vellum on which scribes wrote the Scriptures and other manuscripts.

The Israelites sometimes skinned goats "cased," that is, without cutting the skin down the belly. By tying shut the leg openings and sewing shut the neck and back end, one could use the skin as a bag to carry water or milk. Occasionally the tanners removed the hair by laying the skin in warm water till the hair loosened. At other times they left it on for extra wearing quality. A limited amount of evaporation through the pores of the skin helped to keep the water inside the bag reasonably cool.

When hung inside the tent, empty and exposed to heat and smoke, such skin bottles tended to dry, shrink, and crack (Ps. 119:83). Old bottles could not hold new wine, as Jesus reminded His hearers in Matthew 9:17, for it was likely to expand and burst them. The Gibeonites, when they wanted to make a peace treaty with Joshua under the pretense that they were from a far country, took moldy bread and old, patched bottles to show that they had traveled far (Joshua 9:13).

The Israelites employed goatskins in making bread. They spread a circular piece of goatskin out on the floor and kneaded dough on it. On their last night in Egypt, as they prepared to travel after their Passover meal, they rolled up their dough in such "kneading troughs" and carried it with them.

The Hebrews frequently used the goat as a sacrifice. On the Day of Atonement they selected two goats, the Lord's goat and the scapegoat. The first was sacrificed, and the high priest sprinkled its blood on the mercy seat in the Most Holy Place of the tabernacle. The scapegoat had the accumulated sins of the congregation placed on its head, and then "a fit man" led it to a "land not inhabited" and turned it loose (Lev. 16:20-22). Goats being what they are, the scapegoat probably made a good living for himself in the wilderness, or else found his way back home again.

GOAT, WILD—see Ibex

GREYHOUND—see Dog

HAMSTER—see Mouse

Northern Hare

Syrian Hare

HARE, EGYPTIAN (arnebeth); *Lepus capensis aegyptus*. L 20"
HARE, IRAQI; *Lepus europeus connori*. L 22"
HARE, SYRIAN; *Lepus syriacus*. L 22"

In the case of the hare, even though the Bible mentions it only once, no one disagrees about the animal intended. Deuteronomy 14:7 names it with the coney, classed as unclean meat because the hare chews its cud but doesn't divide the hoof. Actually neither animal chews the cud, but both appear to do so. While sitting still they often move their jaws from side to side as if they are chewing, when they are really sharpening their teeth. When resting, hares drop pellets that are of coarser texture than usual. These they pick up, rechew, and digest over again to obtain additional nourishment. Although one could regard such behavior as a form of chewing the cud, hares still are not ruminants.

The Levitical laws had in mind a people not scientifically educated, and had to speak to them in a way that they would understand. The authors of the Bible did not write it as a science textbook. As we have stated elsewhere, the Levitical prohibitions against certain meats follow no consistent scientific principles, but in some cases there may be health reasons behind them. For instance, hares act as intermediary hosts of the dog tapeworm, which can also live in humans who eat hares.

The Iraqi and Syrian hares that inhabit Palestine are similar to the European hare except they are paler and have shorter ears and a wider head. The Egyptian hare of the southern deserts has a smaller body and large ears.

Hares usually rest in "forms," which are body-sized depressions they have scratched in sheltered spots next to shrubs or grass clumps. Here they squat securely camouflaged against the keen eyesight of eagles, owls, foxes, jackals, and wolves. When surprised by an enemy, they can suddenly leap forward and dash off at a rate of nearly 40 miles an hour.

Young hares are furred, have their eyes open, and can run only a few hours after birth. Rabbits are smaller, shorter-eared, and have large litters of blind and hairless young usually born in underground dens. The range of rabbits does not extend to the Holy Land. They prefer the habitat of the more temperate woodlands of Europe.

HART—see Deer

HEDGEHOG—see Porcupine

HEIFER—see Cattle

HIND—see Deer

HIPPOPOTAMUS; behemoth (behema); *Hippopotamus amphibus.* L 14'

Scholars now generally recognize the behemoth mentioned in Job as being based on the hippopotamus. The "river horse," as the Greeks later named it, was the largest land mammal that the Bible writers were familiar with. It was evidently quite common in the Nile River, and records indicate that it inhabited the Orontes River, in Syria, around 1500 B.C. It may have dwelt in the Jordan during early Bible times, but scholars generally believe that the reference to Jordan is poetic and could mean any river.

The passage in Job 40:15-24 is the only biblical allusion to behemoth, but it gives a fairly complete picture of it. It eats grass as an ox—the hippo lives largely on coarse swamp grass, about 150 pounds a day, and bites it off as an ox does. The elephant picks it with his trunk and stuffs it into his mouth.

Behemoth's strength is in his loins. The hippo looks fat and flabby, but is a powerful animal. Extremely muscular, it can run as fast as a man for short distances. In the water it is as graceful as a ballerina.

The reference to the mountains bringing it food in verse 20 seems to favor the elephant. However, the term *mountain*, as used in the Scriptures, can mean any slight elevation such as a hill. The raised banks along the Nile were prime farming areas. The hippopotamuses ranged out from the river as much as five miles at night, and the gardens of the farmers provided them much food. So much, indeed, that the Romans, when they ruled Egypt, encouraged the hunting of the huge beasts because they made such inroads on the farmer's crops.

The hippo loves nothing better than lying under shady trees and reeds in the water. On hot days it spends hours with only its nostrils, eyes, and ears exposed. This allows it to breathe, see, and hear, even though the rest of the body is submerged in water.

When so many factors point to the hippopotamus, we wonder why the translators of the KJV did not give it that name. One reason could be that a knowledge of the animal was just beginning to reach northern Europe during the 1600s, when the Authorized Version came out. It is quite probable that the English translators had not yet heard of it. We do not always take into account the fact that knowledge spread rather slowly during the Dark Ages and for some time after the invention of printing.

The hippopotamus could be said to have cloven hooves as a pig, but it is more accurate to say that it has a four-toed foot. While it does not chew the cud, it does have three stomachs to help it digest the coarse fare on which it dines. A large adult may be as long as 15 feet and weigh as much as four tons. That makes it twice as heavy as a large workhorse. It has large molars, like those of the elephant, that keep growing during its lifespan of around 40 years. In the front of its mouth four large tusks fit into opposite cavities when the jaws close. The lower tusks project forward and help the animal dig in the ground for tubers and roots. The mouth is so large and the jaws so powerful that they can crush a boat with a man in it.

The early Egyptians, as a painting of them shows, hunted hippos from raft boats by harpooning them. A float at the end of the harpoon rope allowed them to locate the animal even if it dived. They speared it till it died and could be pulled to land. Also they trapped it in pits dug in hippo trails and lightly covered with vegetation. Still another method was to hang a heavily weighted spear above its trail that the hippo would release when it tripped a rope.

The ancients ate the meat of the hippopotamus and rendered the fat for a variety of uses. The hide, cut into long strips, was braided into whips called khoorbashes. These were the whips that Egyptian taskmasters used on the Hebrews.

HOG—see Swine

HORSE (sus, rekesh, 'abbir); *Equus caballus.* H 60″

"Hast thou given the horse strength? hast thou clothed his neck with thunder? Canst thou make him afraid as a grasshopper? the glory of his nostrils is terrible. He paweth in the valley, and rejoiceth in his strength" (Job 39:19-21).

Other translations may render this passage more accurately, but none so poetically or with such grandeur. In the rhetorical questions that God asks of Job it appears that He must have taken special pleasure in the creation of this animal.

The early patriarchs did not know the horse as a domestic animal, and it does not appear as part of their other livestock, not even that of Job to whom God addressed the above question. They must have been wild then, but evidently tamed soon after.

The Arabian horse apparently originated from the southern race of the tarpan, or forest horse, that once roamed wild over most of Europe and Asia Minor. The last tarpan perished in the Ukraine in 1880 when it stepped into a rodent hole during a chase while the people there celebrated the Russian New Year. The forest horse lived in other areas besides the forest, but received its name to distinguish it from the Przewalski's horse of the Mongolian deserts that still exists in zoos. Lighter in build than the Mongolian, the forest horse was a uniform mouse-gray in color with a black mane and tail and a black stripe running down its back. The mane and tail of the primitive animal were fairly short.

Mankind probably first domesticated the horse in Asia Minor or the Euphrates Valley about the time Abraham left Ur of the Chaldees. It was used chiefly in war, which seems to have been the main occupation of the kings of that time. The Hyksos kings, when they overran Egypt, brought the horse into Egypt. The first mention of the horse in the Bible is that of Joseph riding in Pharaoh's second chariot as prime minister of the country. Whether the Hebrews themselves ever used horses in Egypt or not, Scripture does not say, but they evidently did not bring any with them when they left. In Deuteronomy 17:16 Moses warned the people not to multiply horses to themselves or to return to Egypt for more. When the Israelites left Egypt, Pharaoh pursued them with chariots and horsemen, but the animals drowned in the waters of the sea.

The Israelites kept the command of Moses for a while. As they fought with other nations they killed all their horses or houghed them (cut their Achilles' tendons). However, in a battle with Hadadezer, David saved enough horses for 100 chariots (2 Sam. 8:4). After him, Solomon greatly increased his horses and chariots, getting the animals from Egypt.

Some chariots from Egypt have survived, and we also have pictures of ones from later kingdoms. It is interesting to note that chariots changed little through the years. There was no such thing as planned obsolescence then, or putting out a new model every year as we do now with cars. Basically they were wooden boxes, rounded at the front and open at the back, mounted on two wheels with a pole in front. Lighter in weight than those on the earlier carts, the wheels had spokes. The wheels could come off the axles at critical times, as we find recorded in Exodus 14:25. Along the side of the chariot a quiver for arrows was fastened, and in front was a tube for the spear.

Breastbands hitched the horses to the pole in front. The horse had no traces or tugs for pulling, except on much later Roman models that employed three horses in their chariot races. The driver controlled the horses by a bit in the mouth held in place by a leather bridle and guided by reins. Should only one occupant use the chariot, he would fasten the reins around his waist when fighting or hunting. In this way he could control his team by twisting his body and still have his hands free to use a bow or spear. He tied his whip to his wrist so that he would not lose it while in action.

The floor of the chariot often consisted of latticed leather straps that supplied a bit of spring to it. It seems to be the only effort made to make the rider comfortable. A chariot did not have any springs and most of them not even a seat. On a long journey the occupants had to stand all the way.

Even though chariot builders provided little for comfort, they did do quite a bit in the way of ornamentation. The chariot was then, as now, a status symbol, and each one had to try to make his a bit more showy and ostentatious than his neighbor's. Chariots had a lot of gold and silver decoration on them. The horses wore feather crests and tinkling bells on their bridles. The harness, also adorned with gold and silver, was as fancy as it could be.

Drivers at that time were known by their daring and skill, even as they are now. When Joram, king of Israel and son of Ahab and Jezebel, was in Jezreel recovering from wounds received in a battle with the Syrians, he saw a company of soldiers approaching the city. After two of his peace messengers did not return, he looked again, and his watchman said, "The driving is like the driving of Jehu the son of Nimshi; for he driveth furiously" (2 Kings 9:20). He was right.

Chariots also had peaceful purposes, as when Joseph in his chariot supervised the Egyptians or Absalom rode around deceiving his father's subjects. But most of the time they served as military weapons. To foot soldiers the charging charioteers must have been a dreadful sight as they crashed into the soldiers' lines. Sometimes charioteers fixed knives to the wheels to cause even more damage.

It seems strange that with all the references to horses in the earlier books of the Bible there is little mention of anyone riding them. Miriam sang, "The horse and his rider hath he thrown into the sea" (Gen. 15:21). But she apparently referred to the chariot driver or rider. Another reference (1 Kings 20:20) has the Assyrian king escaping "on an horse with horsemen," but the following verse indicates that they rode chariots. In Genesis 49:17 we read of Dan, the adder "that biteth the horse heels, so that his rider shall fall backward." And 2 Kings 9:18, 19 tells of two messengers "on horseback" sent to meet Jehu. Also Ezekiel 23:6 speaks of "desirable young men, horsemen riding upon horses." Then too in Esther 6:11 we find that Haman, much to his chagrin, had to lead a horse with Mordecai on it through the streets of the city. It appears also from archaeological records that the Assyrians rode horses before the Israelites generally did. The latter used asses, mules, and camels as mounts, but they usually *drove* horses. Just why is not altogether clear.

It was not till adoption of the Arabian horse that the animal's full glory and usefulness became fully evident. Its increased maneuverability, coupled with its fleetness of foot on uneven ground, was a real asset.

The Arabs prized mares above stallions as steeds, for the former were more devoted and dependable. The desert tribesmen valued the horse not only for its physical strength and endurance but for its spirit and grit. Arab horsemen rigorously selected their stock and kept only the offspring of the best ones as prize Kochlani. They would ride a young mare at a gallop for 50 miles, make it swim through a river, and then feed her. If she refused to eat, they rejected her as unfit to be called a Kochlani. These intelligent horses were trained not only to come when called, but to stop if the rider fell off and to wait for him. In one case when a rider tumbled off his horse during battle, the animal grabbed him by his clothes and dragged him to a place of safety. An Arab would not sell such a horse. He would sooner part with his wife or another member of his family than to do that.

Arab horses went about unshod. Their hooves were so hard that they did not need shoeing. The Bible has much to say about the flinty hooves of horses, comparing them also to iron and brass. The horses themselves could stand a lot of hard work and abuse when necessary. One Arabian, carrying nearly a third of its own weight, ran 310 miles in 49 hours. Another one stood on board a ship for 100 days without once lying down, then won a race shortly after landing.

That the horses sometimes had to exhibit exceptional endurance does not say that their masters were generally cruel to them. At home their owners treated them like pets or members of the family, even bringing them into the tent. They received choice food, including fresh, warm camel's milk.

The tarpan, ancestor of the Arab horse, was mouse-gray in color, but its descendants came in several shades and colors. They could be dark bay, chestnut, dappled gray in varying shades, nutmeg roan, black, or white with a black skin. The latter are black at birth and turn white as they age. A pure white horse at birth is an albino. Arab horses also had long, luxuriant manes and tails in contrast to the tarpan's short ones.

HYENA, STRIPED (sabua); *Hyaena striata.* L 40"

"Is this land of mine a hyena's lair, with birds of prey hovering all around it?" (NEB). In Jeremiah 12:9 the prophet laments the fate of Israel. The KJV translates the Aramaic *sabua* to read "speckled bird," but the words mean "streaked," and some newer versions read "hyena." It fits the context much better. One can visualize hyenas feeding on the remains of the lion's kill, and the vultures sitting around waiting for their share.

The KJV of Isaiah 13:22 and 34:14—"beasts of the island(s)"—appears as "hyenas" in the Revised Standard Version. The translation of the word *sabua* in the apocryphal book Ecclesiasticus 13:18 as "hyena" would lend weight to the above. "Valley of Zeboim" in 1 Samuel 13:18 could also be rendered "valley of the hyenas." So we see that even though the word *hyena* does not appear in the KJV, it could well have.

The striped hyena has been common in Palestine until recently, and it was even more so during Bible times. For this reason we can expect that Scripture should at least allude to it. Though a creature of the night, and often living in desolate places, it also roamed near towns and cities. Its characteristic tracks of a big forepaw and a small hind one often dotted the sand.

In the times of autocratic kings, when life was cheap, governments and rulers often executed people and left their bodies in the streets to decay. The stench and risk of disease must have been great. It would have been even worse if at night the hyenas did not come and help the dogs devour the carcasses. Many times hyenas lived near graveyards and dug up the bodies of the dead. The rich buried their deceased in tombs hewn out of the rock and blocked by large stones to keep the dogs and hyenas out.

The spotted hyena of Africa often hunts in packs and kills many of the larger game animals. A large enough group will even dispute its prey with a lion. The striped hyena will more likely hunt alone and lives mostly on carrion and small animals. The spotted ones will indulge in hilarious calls that sound like maniacal laughter after a kill, but the striped species usually remains silent.

Hyenas have exceptionally powerful jaws that can crack even the leg bones of a cow, and their digestive system can accommodate chunks and splinters of bone that would make a dog vomit.

Both Arabs and Jews hate and despise the hyena, not only for its grave-robbing proclivities but also for its apparent cowardliness and for the foul smell that attends it. The stench results partly from its diet and partly from scent glands similar to those of most members of the weasel family. In spite of this, it really does a good service to people in getting rid of refuse that would otherwise pollute the air and scenery. In some villages the animals clean up the garbage dumps every night.

Young hyenas usually stay in the home den till they are able to run around. They nurse and remain with their mother for nearly a year after birth. At first their stripes are so wide that they appear to be almost black, but as the hyenas get older the stripes narrow, and in the adult the overall effect is of a gray creature that blends into the shadows of the night.

People sometimes tanned the skins of hyenas by rubbing the flesh side with salt and soaking them in the saline waters of the Dead Sea. Sandals and leggings made from them supposedly have power to protect the wearer from the bite of a hyena.

HYRAX, SYRIAN; coney; rock badger (shaphan); *Hyrax syriacus*. L 20″

"The conies are but a feeble folk, yet make they their houses in the rocks" (Prov. 30:26).

Translators of *The New English Bible* did little to improve the accuracy of the KJV when they referred to the animals as "rock badgers" as opposed to the latter's "conies." They are neither conies (an old name for rabbits) nor badgers, but hyraxes. Biological classifications have placed them in an order by themselves between the sea cows and the elephants, not too far removed from the rhinoceroses and the hippopotamuses. Most people thought this rock dweller was a rabbit because it has similar habits, is near the same size and color, and lives on vegetation. It has large incisors, as do rodents, and would seem to be related to them and the hares and rabbits, but it is not.

The reason for this is in the feet, say the scientists. The front feet have four toes and the hind three, but their nails are flat and resemble small hooves, placing them with the hoofed mammals. The pads under the toes are moist and rubbery, and the creature can raise the center pad to provide suction. Such behavior enables the hyrax to run surefootedly over slippery rocks and climb almost vertical surfaces. It seems a bit odd that the small hyrax should have even a distant relationship to the giant elephant, but some of the fossil hyraxes were nearly as big as horses.

The Syrian hyrax is a gray-brown, furry, short-necked, shortlegged, short-tailed animal about the size of a big groundhog that lives in clans on rocky knolls and hillsides. It burrows between and under boulders and finds a safe refuge there from eagles, leopards, and bears. Hyraxes are social animals. The colonies feed during the day, and one of the group always acts as a lookout, giving a shrill scream of warning in case of danger. Hyraxes eat mostly grass, leafy plants, bulbs, and locusts. They have a scent gland on the back surrounded by lighter-colored hairs that stand erect when anything arouses the animal. The scent helps one who has wandered too far to find the group again. It also aids in attracting a mate.

Females give birth to from three to six young in a season, and the babies can run about shortly after birth. The offspring nurse for about six months. The gestation period for these rabbit-sized mammals is seven and one-half months, while that for a rabbit is only one month. The young are quite playful and love to chase each other around boulders. Such behavior is part of their training for life, but playfulness is also generally a sign of intelligence. They are quite noisy and whistle, chatter, and scream at each other.

The Bible mentions the coney only four times. Leviticus 11:5 and Deuteronomy 14:7 both refer to it as being unclean because though it chews the cud, it does not divide the hoof. Actually, as with the hare, it does not chew the cud but only appears to. While resting, it often grinds its jaws sideways to keep the molars sharp-edged and to hone the large incisors to a chisel edge. Such grinding also prevents the constantly growing incisors from becoming too long.

The other two references, Psalm 104:18 and Proverbs 30:26, commend the coney for its intelligence in choosing the high rocks for its refuge even though it is otherwise a feeble and defenseless animal.

Several species of hyraxes inhabit Africa east of the Sahara. The Syrian hyrax occupies the northern end of the creature's range. Many others, called dassies by the Africans, live in the small, rocky outcroppings known as kopjes on the African plains. Hyraxes used to be quite numerous, but have become less common because of the demand for their furs in making coats.

In the western mountains of North America dwells a small mammal often referred to as a coney. It is not related to the hyraxes of the Old World, but to the rabbits, and thus we can correctly call it a rock rabbit though its real name is pica. Like the biblical coney, it also inhabits the rocks, preferring the jumble of a rockslide where it can retreat to its nest far down between the loosely piled boulders. Feeding on grass and flowers, it dries them in the sun and stores them underground for the winter, where it feeds contentedly on its private hay pile far beneath the deep mountain snows.

IBEX, NUBIAN; wild goat (ya'el, 'aqqo) (eriphos); *Capra Ibex nubiana.* H 36"

"The high hills are a refuge of the wild goats" (Ps. 104:18).

When David hid in the hills of Judea, he became well acquainted with the wild goats of the region. Without doubt the Hebrew term *ya'el*, which means "climber," refers to the Nubian ibex in the Scriptures. The animal greatly resembles the Alpine ibex, or steinbok, except that the Nubian has a black beard, and horns that have three angles instead of four. The general color is gray and black, with white underneath. It is browner in winter. The magnificent horns of the male, though more slender than those of the steinbok, sweep backward in a wide curve, and may be up to 50 inches long. Females have smaller ones.

The goats live together in small flocks in the rocky hills. In Bible times they were quite common in the Judean hills at the southern end of the Dead Sea, and around En-gedi (Fountain of Goats), where David found a refuge when he fled from Saul. They are agile and surefooted, even though they carry heavy horns. With their keen eyesight, their sentries spot danger a long way off and warn the rest with a shrill whistle.

The flesh of such wild goats is said to be excellent eating. Since few deer inhabit the southern deserts around Beer-sheba, where Isaac lived, some have suggested that the "venison" that Isaac asked his oldest son to get for him in preparation for receiving the birthright might have been from the ibex. When Jacob appeared with the savory meat from domestic kids, Isaac expressed surprise that he should have found it so quickly (Gen. 27:20).

Isaiah 13:21 and 34:14 speaks in eloquent, poetic terms of the fall of Babylon, stating that wild beasts would inhabit its ruins "and satyrs shall dance there," also "the satyr shall cry to his fellow." Bible scholars feel that since the other animals mentioned in the passages are literal, the *sa'ir*, or hairy creature, should be rendered "wild goat" rather than satyr. It may well be so, for the Hebrew prophet would hardly have referred here to the half-man, half-goat creature of Greek mythology.

Even though man has brought the wild goats of Bible lands to near extinction, government authorities now protect them in a wildlife sanctuary near En-gedi.

IVORY—see Elephant

JACKAL, GOLDEN (shual, tan, tannim) (alopex); *Canis aureus.* H 36″. See also Fox.

Without doubt *shual*, the term for fox in Hebrew, also referred to the jackal in Bible times. The jackal was the big fox, while the others were the "little foxes." It is interesting to note that the word "jackal" was just becoming known in England about the year 1600, and Bible scholars were probably not yet aware of it at the time of the translation of the Authorized Version of the Bible. That may explain why the term does not appear in the KJV, even though a number of times *shual* quite obviously refers to it, and later versions rendered it that way.

The jackal's coat is a dirty yellow with some tufts of red and black in it. Its tail is not bushy like that of the fox, nor is its fur as long. The nose is more pointed than that of most dogs, but some have argued that it is one of the ancestors of some breeds of domestic canines.

Jackals were plentiful in Palestine during the early days. They slept in dens in rocky places, graveyards, or ruins during the day, then at night they would gather into big packs of up to several hundred to scavenge for food. They lived mostly on carrion. As the dogs of the time performed the role of a sanitary commission in the towns and cities, so the jackals did that work in the country. With the aid of vultures and their own keen noses, they found any animals that died and devoured their remains. Jackals trailed hunters around and cleaned up after their kills.

After a battle the jackals had a field day (or rather night), feasting along with the hyenas and vultures on the casualties, picking clean the bones of the dead. Any casual reading of the Old Testament makes it plain that there must have been many such occasions.

The 300 "foxes" that Samson sent through the grainfields of the Philistines with firebrands tied between their tails must certainly have been jackals. He could have trapped that many in a baited enclosure without too much difficulty, whereas it would have been extremely difficult for him to catch that many real foxes. They are most always found singly and are extremely wary.

Samson did not actually tie the firebrands to the jackals' tails, but to a cord between a pair of them. Then, as they ran this way and that through the fields, they set large acreages on fire. It was a fiendish revenge, and we tend to recoil at it and to sympathize with the jackals. But in his time Samson was not unusually cruel to animals, for people kicked and beat even dogs unmercifully. Though blessed with superior strength, Samson was undeniably short on moral sensitivity and compassion (Judges 15:4, 5).

JERBOA—see Mouse

KID—see Goat

KINE—see Cattle

LAMB—see Sheep

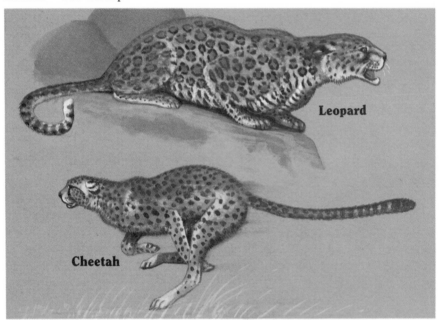

LEOPARD (namer, nemar) (pardalis); *Panthera pardus.* L 60″

"Can the Ethiopian change his skin, or the leopard his spots?" (Jer. 13:23).

The word *leopard* comes from a combination of the two words *leo* and *pardus*. Many people in ancient times thought that this big cat represented a cross between the lion and the panther. The panther then was what we today know to be the black, or melanistic, phase of the leopard that may appear in any litter with spotted siblings. Leopards have a wide distribution throughout most of Africa and southern Asia. They were fairly common in Palestine in Bible times and lived there until quite recently. A female and cub were killed there in 1962.

Though weighing only 100 to 200 pounds and smaller than either the lion or the tiger, the leopard is a powerful animal and can drag a kill weighing as much as it does up into the crotch of a tree. Fond of being in trees, it can climb them easily. It will often lie in wait on a limb over a game trail and leap on the back of a passing antelope or deer. Scripture alludes to the animal's trait of lying in wait, often on a rock near a trail, in Jeremiah 5:6: "A leopard shall watch over their cities; every one that

63

goeth out thence shall be torn in pieces."

Leopards also often sneak up on herds of animals, and dash into them to bring down their prey. They hate to share their kill with hyenas, jackals, or vultures, so they drag it up into a tree to feast in peace and return for more later.

The coat of a leopard is yellowish, covered with black spots that take the form of rosettes on the flanks. The spotted fur has good camouflage value, especially in trees, where the sun casts dappled shadows over everything. Black leopards also have spots, but because they are black on black, you can see them only in good light, confirming Jeremiah's statement, since even a black leopard can't change his spots or get rid of them. Taken out of its natural setting, the fur of a leopard is quite striking. It often formed part of the royal robes of kings.

Leopards prey mostly on antelope and deer, but they will also catch and eat smaller animals such as baboons, monkeys, and various rodents. In settled regions they devour livestock as well. They are especially fond of dogs, or else have a special grudge against them for giving away their presence with their noisy barking. The predators will sneak up on the porch of a house to nab a dog. In fact, they are so sly and quiet about it that they often catch the dog asleep.

Usually leopards do not attack people, but occasionally, as with lions and tigers, one will become a man-killer. Usually it is an old or wounded animal that can no longer compete for wild prey or has a score to even up with man. It has lost none of its cunning, however, and is often difficult to kill.

The word used for leopard in the Bible apparently stood for more different species than it does now. It probably also included the cheetah as well as some of the other cats that lived in the region. The cheetah, which still lives in much of the leopard's range, received special training as a hunter from the Assyrians. Most likely the "leopard" referred to in Habakkuk 1:8—"Their horses also are swifter than the leopards"—was the cheetah. The leopard is fast but does not usually follow its prey very far. The cheetah, one of the fastest animals known, has been clocked at 70 miles per hour. Although about the same size as a leopard, it is more slender and long-legged. It has black spots on a yellowish fur, but the spots are smaller and solid instead of rosette-shaped.

A number of smaller cats also lived in Palestine. The caracal, a desert lynx, still roams the Negev Desert and the coastal plains. The tawny cat has markings only on the face and ears. Reports indicate that the Pallas cat, or sand cat, also ranges into the Negev. Long-tailed, it also has markings only on the face and tail. However, it is quite a bit smaller than the caracal, being not much bigger than a house cat. We have no reason to believe that any of the biblical references have either animal in mind. The spotted fishing cat lives in the Jordan River marshes and now receives government protection. The wildcat, ancestor of the domestic tabby, apparently first underwent domestication in Egypt. The Egyptians embalmed many and even made the animal into a goddess. The Israelites would surely have been acquainted with cats, but if they took some to the Promised Land with them, Scripture does not mention that fact.

LION ('ari, labi, laba, 'aryeh, kephir, layish, shachal, liba'ah, libiya, shachas) (leon); *Panthera leo.* L 65″

"The wicked flee when no man pursueth: but the righteous are bold as a lion" (Prov. 28:1).

Probably no other wild animal receives mention as often in the Bible as does the lion. We find not only one Hebrew term for the animal, but six, as well as one in Greek. Ari means "the strong one." It seems that we have Hebrew words not only for the male, female, and young, but some scholars believe that the two sets of terms refer to the two species of lions that at one time inhabited the region. A smaller variety of the African lion lived in Egypt and the Sinai Peninsula. The Asiatic lion, a shorter-maned animal, roamed much of Palestine, Assyria, Babylon, and northern India. A number of scholars thus believe that the terms *labi, lebiya,* and *sachas* refer to the latter, and *ari, aryeh,* and *kephir* to the former species. Noting the inexactness of many of the Hebrew animal names, however, we see that it would be a bit unusual indeed if that were the case.

The lion has become extinct in Palestine since about the time of the Crusaders. Today only about 200 of the Asiatic lions still survive in the Gir Forest in India. African lions, though more plentiful, live only in scattered locations south of the Sahara Desert.

Lions may hunt alone, but they also gather in prides, or groups of 10 or 20 that include several related females with cubs and three or four adult males. We usually like to think of the heavy-maned male lion as being the king of the jungle, more powerful than any other predator. Actually the animals do not live in the jungle, but in the open plains and scrub country, where they prey on the grazing herds of zebras as well as wildebeests and other antelopes. The male lion is a lazy parasite who spends most of his time sleeping. The females are the daring hunters and kill game for the pride. The lordly male then takes his share after the kill. If the pride has plenty of food, the cubs get some of the bounty, but if not, they often starve. The lioness does not show as much concern for the welfare of her cubs as does a mother bear.

Throughout much of the early history of the Israelites, lions were evidently quite plentiful, and herdsmen had to defend their flocks and themselves against the powerful predators. Many Scripture texts indicate that it was common for a lion to attack a man. When the Assyrians replaced the inhabitants of the northern kingdom with people from other Babylonian provinces (2 Kings 17:23-28), lions increased so much that the new settlers complained to the king about it. Their gods, it seemed, were unable to protect them from the animals. The Assyrian ruler had to import a Hebrew priest to teach them about their God, who could protect them.

Since the coming of firearms lions have learned to have a healthy respect for people, and do not attack them except in rare instances when one becomes a man-killer through old age, loss of teeth, or other disability. Then it becomes especially wary and is often hard to deal with.

The ultimate feat of bravery for a man of Bible times was to kill a lion single-handed. A young lion roared at Samson as he traveled to Timnath with his parents. He tore the predator apart with his bare hands and left the body. Samson must have been separated from his parents at the time, for the record says that he did not tell them about it. They were on their way to make arrangements for him to marry a young Philistine girl. Later he came back that way to claim his bride. Stopping to see the lion carcass, Samson found that wild bees had taken over the remains and built a comb in it. He shared some of the honeycomb with his parents but did not tell them where it came from. At the wedding party Samson used the incident to concoct a riddle for the men of the city.

David killed a lion that took a lamb from his flock. He said he grabbed it by its beard (mane) and struck it, probably with a club (1 Sam. 17:34-36). One of David's mighty men, Benaiah, went down into a pit on a snowy day and killed a lion there (2 Sam. 23:20).

Folklore usually looks upon the lion as the epitome of courage and strength, and Scripture often reflects this tradition. In Genesis 49:9 and Numbers 23:24 the lion symbolizes the Jews and the kings that came from them. Revelation 5:5 refers to Christ as the "Lion of the tribe of Judah," a title that the kings of Ethiopia appropriated in their claim as the supposed descendants of David through Solomon and the queen of Sheba. "The righteous are bold as a lion," in our introductory passage, also stresses this thought.

In prophetic symbols the lion depicts strength and glory. Nebuchadnezzar's dream pictures Babylon as a winged lion (Dan. 7:4). John the revelator tells of his vision of heaven and of the four beasts or creatures, the first of them, as recorded in Revelation 4:7, like a lion.

The Bible has emphasized the peacefulness of the earth made new by contrasting the fierce nature of the lion with what it will be like when "no lion shall be there, nor any ravenous beast shall go up thereon" (Isa. 35:9) and "the lion shall eat straw like the ox" (Isa. 11:7).

1 Peter 5:8 brings out another aspect of the lion by comparing it to Satan: "The devil, as a roaring lion, walketh about, seeking whom he may devour."

Lions entered into two curious stories of prophets as told in 1 Kings 13:11-30 and 20:35, 36. The first describes a prophet whom God ordered to deliver a message and to not stop to eat or drink until he returned home. But another prophet, who claimed to have a later message, persuaded him that he should stop and eat with him. The first prophet did. On his way back home a lion came out of the thicket and killed him. It did not eat him or bother the ass that stood near by.

The other story recounts a man ordered by a prophet to strike him in the face. The man refused to do it, and the prophet told him that a lion would kill him. It did.

Hunters sometimes caught lions in pits dug in trails and lightly covered with brush. Kings kept them in stone-walled enclosures or dens for the amusement of their courts. It apparently pleased them to have power over such fierce animals. Sometimes they pitted the lions against other animals in fights or used the beasts to execute political prisoners. Daniel's enemies contrived to have him thrown into the den of lions, but the scheme backfired. The lions did not touch Daniel, but later tore his enemies to pieces after the king had them hurled among the creatures.

People also snared lions in nets. Several heavy nets would be propped up so that a lion, driven into them by dogs, would become entangled as they fell over him. Then the hunters could take the animal alive.

Roman emperors loved to entertain themselves and their subjects by arena spectaculars in which captured Christians had to confront starving lions. Paul says in 2 Timothy 4:17, "I was delivered out of the mouth of the lion." The authorities may have condemned him to be thrown to the lions and then given him a reprieve. It is also quite likely that Paul is speaking figuratively and referring to deliverance from the forces of evil.

MANATEE—see Dugong

MOLE RAT (chephar-parath); *Spalax typhlus.* L 10″

Palestine has no moles, but the animal designated by the Hebrew *chephar-parath* and translated as mole in the KJV is most likely the mole rat. It is common there and also around the Black Sea and a number of eastern Mediterranean countries. The true mole is an insectivore, related to the shrews and bats, and is in an entirely different order of classification than the mole rat.

Mole rats are rodents, related to mice, ground squirrels, beavers, and porcupines. It is probably most similar to the pocket gophers of America in appearance and habits, about eight inches long with a big head and stocky body joined by an almost nonexistent neck. The creature has no visible eyes or ears, and the head appears quite featureless except for the two pairs of prominent rodent teeth that protrude forward from the large mouth. The legs are short but heavy, and the feet have large claws. Because the animal constantly uses them in digging, the front legs have especially powerful muscles. The rudimentary tail probably serves only as a sensory organ as the animal feels its way backward in its dark tunnels. The mole rat is entirely blind, the vestigial eyes being covered with skin, but its hearing is acute in spite of the absence of visible outer ears. A thick, soft and plushlike yellowish-brown to light slate-colored fur covers the body. The plushlikeness enables the animal to go forward or backward in its tunnels without rubbing the fur the wrong way. The color of the fur usually corresponds to that of the soil in which it lives.

Since the mole rat sleeps during the day and works mostly at night, underground at that, it probably does not need eyesight. It usually lives in light, rich soil that has moisture enough to support vegetation. Here it digs many shallow tunnels, pushing up the earth in mounds along its route. On the way it eats the roots of plants it encounters. The creature is especially fond of the bulbs, tubers, and fleshy roots common to plants growing in a land where they need to store food and water through a dry season. If the mole rat should happen to dig in a garden and run into a row of carrots, onions, or potatoes, it could do quite a bit of damage. Most of the time, in uncultivated soil, it helps destroy weeds, encourages grasses with their fibrous roots, and aerates and mixes the earth with its many tunnels.

About 15 different species of mole rats range from India to southern Africa. Most of them are smaller than the Palestinian species, and most of them also have proportionally longer tails. In southern Africa lives the naked mole rat. It has whiskers and only a few hairs on its pink body and looks like a wrinkled wiener with legs. However its eyes are open, and its ears are visible. These mole rats congregate in colonies and dig their tunnels cooperatively, several of them helping to move the earth along.

The one reference to moles in the Bible (Isa. 2:20) says that men shall throw their idols of silver and gold "to the moles and to the bats." We may wonder what the two animals have in common. In the Holy Land, however, mole rats often inhabit the rich ground around ruins, graveyards, and dumps, places where one also finds bats. Here, where people discard worn-out or broken things, they would also abandon their useless idols.

MONGOOSE—see Weasel

MONKEY (qoph); *Macaca sylvana* or *Cercopithecus pygerythrus*. L 22″

The Bible mentions apes only twice, and in both instances scholars tell us the word should have been monkey rather than ape. The parallel texts of 1 Kings 10:22 and 2 Chronicles 9:21 refer to the cargo of Solomon's ships that included apes, peacocks, gold, silver, and ivory. Because of the peacocks, many once thought that the ships must have come from India or Ceylon. In that case the most probable monkeys would have been the rhesus, the hanuman langur, or the lion-tailed baboon.

Now more recent studies seem to indicate that the Hebrew word *tuki* translated as "peacock" really means another kind of monkey, or maybe even a female. In this case the ships of Solomon and Hiram could have brought items from the coast of northern Africa or down the Red Sea as far as Somaliland. They could have been Barbary apes, which are actually tailless monkeys; or vervet monkeys, one species of a big tribe of guenons that live mostly in central Africa.

Since Solomon had a great interest in natural history, it probably gave him pleasure to have around him some of the curious animals of other countries that his sailors had told him about. We have no record of either apes or monkeys having lived in Palestine during Bible times. That would account for the fact that the Bible does not mention this large order of mammals any more than it does.

MOUFLON—see Aoudad

MOUSE, FIELD; vole (akbar); *Microtus.* L 5″
GERBIL; *Gerbillus aegyptiacus.* L 5 1/2″
MOUSE, HARVEST; *Micromys minutus.* L 3″
HAMSTER; *Cricetus cricetus.* L 7″
MOUSE, SPINY-BACKED; *Acomy.* L 3″
JERBOA; *Jaculus aegyptiacus.* L 6″
DORMOUSE; *Muscardinus avellanarius. L 3″*
RAT, BLACK; *Rattus rattus.* L 9″

The Hebrew *akbar* probably refers to a number of different Palestinian rodents numerous enough to cause trouble or attract attention in other ways. Leviticus 11:29 classifies it as an unclean animal. The mouse is so small that it would hardly seem to warrant the prohibition, but Arabs ate some of the larger rodents like the jerboa and the dormouse.

The jerboa is common in the desert areas of Palestine and Egypt. A fist-sized rodent with long, powerful hind legs and a long tail, it hops about at night like the kangaroo rats of our western deserts. Isaiah 66:17 tells of people who tried to sanctify themselves by pagan rites and flagrantly ate forbidden things, including the abomination, the mouse. *The New English Bible* translates it as "rats" or "jerboas."

Hamsters, common in the Holy Land, also wound up on the menu. They can multiply rapidly and become a threat to crops. Instead of hibernating in winter, they store grain in underground cells. People have found caches of 70 to 100 pounds of grain in hamster dens. It must have taken a number of animals to accumulate amounts that large, for one pair could hardly have gathered that much, let alone eaten it. Dormice, plump little hibernators, also abound in that area and are eaten.

Gerbils, sand rats, and spiny-backed mice also inhabit the Holy Land. The shrew, even though it is an insectivore and not a rodent, would probably also have been classed as a mouse in those days. However, none of them were numerous or important enough to rate special mention in the Bible.

The harvest mouse looks much like a house mouse but is even smaller. It has a long, tapered tail, large, paper-thin ears, and ranges from buff to orange in color. Quite a climber, it may build its ball-shaped nest, tied to weed and grass stems, five or more feet above the ground. Usually it lives in or near grainfields, and it can become numerous around harvest time, devouring large quantities of grain.

The species of mice that really multiply to plague proportions and cause extensive crop damage are the field mice, or voles. The vole is a short-legged, short-eared, brown-furred creature with a moderately short tail and beady eyes nearly hidden in its fur. It generally lives in long grass or field crops, and makes numerous runways along the ground from its feeding areas to its ball-like nest of grass secreted in brush or in a hole underground. It was likely a vole that the poet Robert Burns turned over with his plow, and sorrowed over in his ode "To a Mouse." Voles are extremely active little animals, eating their own weight in food every 24 hours. Thus the little creature has to hustle along its runways to find that much food.

They can have 16 litters of up to a dozen young in a year, which wean in two weeks and can mate in four. One pair could, theoretically, increase to more than 1 million in a year. Naturally predators, food shortages, and disease prevent this from happening, but under optimum conditions they can become a real plague.

1 Samuel 6:4-18 describes a plague of mice among the Philistines that came as punishment for keeping the captured ark of God in their midst. The plague may have consisted of field mice, or possibly harvest mice, but another factor in the story complicates it and suggests that the "mice" may have been rats.

Ordinary rats, both brown and black, lived in the cities of most of the ancient world then as they do now, but neither of them frequent the harvest fields. They prefer to be near man and to share in his bounties. The black rat is one of the prime carriers of the fleas that host the bubonic plague. It is the feared pestilence that apparently originated in Egypt and swept through the civilizations in ancient times as well as the Middle Ages, when it ravaged Europe and earned the title Black Death. One of the outward distinguishing marks of the plague are the buboes, or enlarged glands in the groin and elsewhere. Some commentators believe that the "emrods" mentioned in connection with the above biblical event were the visible symptoms of the bubonic plague that killed thousands of the Philistines. The epidemic evidently resulted from a heavy infestation of rats in the cities. The infected fleas spread to the people, and large numbers became sick and died. As a propitiation to the Hebrew God the Philistines made golden images of the emrods and of the "mice," one for each of the Philistine cities involved, and presented them to the Israelites with the returned ark.

MULE (pered, the male; pirdah, the female); *Equus asinus-equus.*
H 54"

The mule, a cross between a mare and a male ass, appears a number of times in the Old Testament, but not in the New. The earliest reference to it in the KJV is Genesis 36:24, which speaks of a certain "Ana that found the mules in the wilderness, as he fed the asses of Zibeon his father." The passage seems to point to the original accidental crossing of the horse with the ass to produce hybrid offspring. However, it is disappointing to find that "mules" is just a mistranslation and that it should read "hot springs" or "sulphur springs" instead of "mules."

The first bona fide use of the term *mules* is in regard to King David and his sons, as recorded in 2 Samuel 13 and 18. There we find that David and his sons all rode mules. Absalom lost his life during the battle with Joab (2 Sam. 18:9-14) when his mule ran under an oak (terebinth) in the woods and the prince's long hair caught on an overhanging bough. The mule ran away and left Absalom hanging there at the mercy of Joab, who came along and speared him.

Later, when Solomon's accession to the throne appeared threatened (1

Kings 1:33), David told Zadock the priest to put Solomon on David's mule, which was almost the equivalent of his throne, and to parade him before the people.

Both events took place a few years after the occasion when David, for the first time, saved 200 horses as booty from the defeat of Hadadezer in battle (2 Sam. 8:4). Either he had some of the mares bred to his jackasses to produce mules, or else he imported the mules from Egypt as Solomon later did horses. The latter seems a bit more likely in view of the command in Leviticus 19:19 against the hybridizing of any Israelite livestock.

It is interesting that the mule should have been the favorite royal riding animal rather than the horse, but we must bear in mind that Moses had warned Israel against acquiring horses (Deut. 17:16), and their general use for riding only came later. The mule must have been quite an improvement as a mount over the ass.

Crossing a female ass with a stud horse results in a hinny. The small hybrid does not appear to be much of an improvement over the donkey. The jackass-mare cross, however, produces an offspring that usually has the good points of both parents. The colt gets its long ears, short mane, sparsely-haired tail, narrow hoof, sure-footedness, tough skin, and endurance from the father. From the mother comes the large, well-shaped, muscular body and whatever tractability it may possess. Its voice is neither a bray nor a whinny, and is not as impressive as either. The mule is not likely to overwork itself, but saves its strength for when it is needed.

Mules commonly served as pack animals in later Old Testament times. We read in 2 Kings 5:17 that when Naaman, after he had been healed of leprosy, wanted to worship the true God, he asked for two mule-burdens of soil from Israel to take back to Assyria with him on which he could kneel. The account seems to suggest that a mule's burden represented a unit of weight at that time.

The mule is one domestic animal for which we know of no wild ancestor. Sometimes people speak of it as an animal without a past or a future—no proud ancestry and no descendants. It is rare that a female mule will have an offspring, and still more rare for a male mule to be fertile. Yet there have been some. Despite the fact that mules usually cannot reproduce themselves, they have found a place among the people of Bible times as well as in more recent days.

ONAGER; wild ass ('arad, 'arod); *Equus hemionue onager.* H 48″

"Who has let the wild ass of Syria range at will and given the wild ass of Arabia its freedom?—whose home I have made in the wilderness and its lair in the saltings; it disdains the noise of the city and is deaf to the driver's shouting; it roams the hills as its pasture and searches for anything green" (Job 39:5-8, NEB).

The onager, known in the Scriptures as the wild ass, lived in the deserts of Persia and Palestine during the biblical period and was apparently well known to the author of Job. The Sumerians, as we know from drawings on tablets they left, trained onagers to pull four-wheeled chariots. They caught them with lassos, led them by nose rings, and drove them with a muzzle bridle and reins as they drove donkeys. After the domestication of horses, people no longer used onagers.

Several wild asses exist today, or have until recent times. Besides the onagers, kulans roam Mongolia and kiangs in Tibet. Hunting has reduced both to near extinction. There are also the long-eared wild asses of northern Africa, ancestors of the domestic donkey, that also have become nearly extinct. The burros in the American southwestern states are not really wild but feral, being the descendants of escaped domesticated stock.

In earlier times man hunted onagers for their meat. In spite of the barrenness of the land in which they live, these asses usually seem to be in good condition, and the ancients considered their flesh quite tasty. It was, however, forbidden to the Jews. Onagers are exceptionally wary, preferring the freedom of their wide, open spaces. Fleet of foot, they are hard to run down. Hunters on the backs of fast camels used to chase them and run big lion dogs after them to pull them down.

The description of the onager in Job, quoted above from *The New English Bible,* accurately reflects the animals. Because they love their freedom, they live on salt, or alkali, flats in the remote wilderness. They ignore the shouts of the drivers for, in spite of what the Sumerian tablets portray, they are considered nearly untamable. Even the young cannot be trained to bear burdens or to pull a plow. They roam the hills in bands looking for any green thing to eat. Job 6:5 refers to this fact: "Doth the wild ass bray when he hath grass?"

In Genesis 16:12 the angel of the Lord tells Hagar that her son "shall be a man like the wild ass, his hand against every man and every man's hand against him" (NEB). Jeremiah 2:24 describes the Jewish nation as "a wild ass used to the wilderness, that snuffeth up the wind at her pleasure." The passage gives us a quite different picture of the onager than that of the domesticated donkey, the slow-plodding servant of man.

ORYX, ARABIAN (te'o); *Oryx leucoryx*. H 40″

"As a wild bull [oryx] in a net: they are full of the fury of the Lord" (Isa. 51:20).

Scripture alludes to this creature only twice. The other quote, in Deuteronomy 14:5, lists it among the clean animals that the Jews could eat. The fact that in the latter context it appears distinct from the true cattle indicates that it is likely not a *bull,* as the KJV translates it. More recent versions refer to it as an antelope. Scholars who have given particular attention to the natural history of the Bible feel convinced that it is the oryx, a large antelope. The text quoted above infers that it is big and powerful.

The Arabian oryx occupied Palestine during Bible times. Hunters caught it by driving it into a hemp net up to 13 feet wide and fastened down at the bottom across a gully. Riders or beaters drove the animals ahead of them, and as the creatures tried to escape through the ravine, they ran into the net which fell over them, and the more they tried to free themselves, the more securely their long horns and legs became entangled in the net.

The species of oryx that lived in Palestine is the smallest of the four that now exist, but it is still three to four feet tall at the shoulder. The gemsbok of Africa is the largest, averaging four feet tall. The Arabian oryx is the only one of the four found outside of Africa. Living in the hottest and driest deserts, its body is grayish white with dark legs, horns, and facial markings. Both male and female have long, slender, curving horns. The other oryxes all have horns that are as straight as daggers. While not as fast as some, these antelopes are formidable fighters and have been known to kill lions at times.

Like the addax, the oryx can go for long periods without drinking water. Evidently, like the kangaroo rat, it can make water out of the carbohydrates in its food. The antelope browses on desert shrubs, digs up tubers, and enjoys green grass when it is available. Inhabiting the desert, it usually sleeps in the shade during the day, chewing its cud, then comes out to feed at night. It herds together with others of its kind, if it can find them. This species of oryx is now almost extinct, the last one in North Africa being killed in 1906. Only a few still remain in Saudi Arabia, where the government now protects them. Zoos around the world contain a few, and a number have been taken to Arizona for breeding purposes in an attempt to preserve the species.

OXEN—see Cattle

OX, WILD—see Aurochs

PIG—see Swine

PORCUPINE (qippod); *Hystrix cristata.* L 16"
HEDGEHOG; *Erinaceus europaeus.*

There may be no valid reason for including the porcupine here because the translation of the Hebrew *qippod* as "porcupine" in the Revised Standard Version of the Bible is doubtful. However, the word "bittern" in the KJV, or "bustard" in *The New English Bible*, is not much better. The word appears in Isaiah 14:23, 34:11, and Zephaniah 2:14, and the context seems to indicate that the creatures, especially in Zephaniah, perched upon the capitals of the pillars of ruined buildings. The porcupines of North and South America climb trees, and some practically live in them, but the Old World crested porcupine is strictly a ground dwelling animal and would not be likely to climb up a pillar just to sit there. A great digger, it excavates holes to live in. It is fond of vegetables and other plants. The crested porcupine has needles nearly a foot long. They are not barbed, however, like those of the New World species, and for that reason are easier to extract.

The RSV also translates *qippod* as "hedgehog." Both animals may have gone by that name, since both have quills. The two are, of course, not related. The porcupine is a rodent, living on bark, roots, grain, and plants, while the hedgehog is an insectivore, related to the moles and shrews. It eats reptiles, insects, and bird eggs. The crested porcupine lives in the Holy

Land, and three species of hedgehog also dwell there. One, similar to the European species, inhabits the northern parts, and two species live in the southern deserts. They are nocturnal in their habits and also terrestrial, preferring to stay on the ground. When threatened they automatically roll up into a prickly ball. While such behavior is a good defense against most predators, it is not very effective against cars on the highways, and many of the animals meet their end suddenly in this way.

The word *qippod* is probably better translated "tawny owl," and we will deal with it under that heading later in the volume of this series on birds.

PORPOISE—see Dugong

PYGARG—see Addax

RAM—see Sheep

RAT—see Mouse

RATEL; honey badger (tachash); *Mellivora capensis*. L 28″

According to the KJV, badger skins served as the outer covering of the roof of the tabernacle Moses had built in the Sinai Desert (Ex. 25:5; 26:14). The Israelites also used them to protect the various articles of furniture in the tabernacle when the congregation moved from one place to another (Num. 4:10-14)—that is if the Authorized Version has correctly translated the Hebrew word *tachash*. But scholars have considerable doubt about which animal the Bible writer meant. Some believe that it could have been the dugong, or sea cow. We will deal with it under both headings and let the reader choose the one that seems most reasonable.

The range of the European badger does not extend to the Sinai desert where the Hebrews constructed the tabernacle, but it did live in northern Palestine. A related animal, the ratel or honey badger, does live over most of Africa, Arabia, and even India. This would have to be the one that Scripture would have in mind.

The KJV lists badger skins with other items considered precious, such as gold, silver, brass, fine linen, goat's hair, ram skins dyed red, and shittim wood. It seems to indicate that they were also regarded as valuable. Ratels are not common, and it might have been rather difficult for the Israelites to catch enough of them. That alone might make them precious.

Since the skins provided the outer covering on the roof and also served as protective wrappings for the furniture of the tabernacle, they had to be weatherproof and durable. The long guard hair on the furs would have shed rain well, and the black and gray fur would have made a striking pattern on the roof. The badger's hide is tough enough to withstand porcupine quills and the stings of bees as it robs their nests.

Ezekiel 16:10 describes symbolically how the Lord cared for Jerusalem: "I . . . shod thee with badger skin." The fine leather of the tough honey badger would have been in keeping with the rest of the items mentioned in the chapter.

The ratel teams up with a small bird known as the honey guide. The bird calls him and leads him to a nest of wild honey bees. Then after the honey badger has torn open the nest with its powerful claws and eaten its fill of honey and larvae, the bird gets its share of the leftover honey and wax.

Honey badgers prowl mostly at night. They eat a number of kinds of insects, fruit, small rodents, and reptiles as well as bees. Both ratels and other badgers belong to the Mustela family, in which we also find the skunk, weasel, otter, and wolverine. All of them have scent glands, but most of them, including the ratel, can not spray the scent as liberally as does the skunk.

RHINOCEROS—see Unicorn
ROCK BADGER—see Hyrax
ROEBUCK—see Deer, also Gazelle
SATYR—see Ibex

SHEEP (rachel, kebes, 'seh, sona', keseb, so'n, ben so'n, kabsah, kar, kibsah, taleh, teli, immar, soneh) (probaton, pascha, amnos, arnion) *Ovis laticaudata*. H 26"

"We are his people, and the sheep of his pasture" (Ps. 100:3).

Scripture probably mentions no other animal as often as it does the sheep or its progeny. No other is bound up so closely with God's chosen people, none used symbolically so often, and none as often employed to represent Christ. Abel, son of Adam and Eve, is the first one mentioned in the Bible to keep sheep. The patriarchs—Abraham, Isaac, and Jacob —counted their wealth in sheep, as did Job. The children of Israel had large flocks of sheep.

In Abraham's time most of the land where he lived was not owned. That was why he could wander about from place to place with his vast flocks. The river valleys were settled, but even there Lot found pasture for his flocks around the lower Jordan and the cities of Sodom and Gomorrah. Most of the hill country consisted of empty land, and there Abraham lived with his flocks of sheep and cattle. People did own wells and the land around them. No one could draw water from a well unless entitled to it. In

Genesis 21:25 and 26:15, 18-33, we read of the struggles both Abraham and Isaac had over the ownership of wells they had dug. Jacob met his future wife, Rachel, at her father's well and helped water her flocks (Gen. 29:9, 10). Moses also encountered his future wife at her father's well in Midian and helped her water her sheep despite opposition from rival herdsmen (Ex. 2:16-19).

Water was precious to sheepherders, as were green pastures. David, the shepherd king, knew what he was talking about when he wrote in the twenty-third psalm, "He maketh me to lie down in green pastures; he leadeth me beside the still waters." Sheep need water, but when necessary they can go for several days without it.

In general, sheep are stupid, dependent, and defenseless. For that reason the owner must take good care of them. When lambs are born in the field, the shepherd carries them in his arms to shelter. He must protect his flock from enemies. David killed a lion and a bear that tried to seize lambs. The threat of wolves was always there. Thus the Bible has much to say about sheep and wolves. When Christ commissioned His disciples, He said, "Behold, I send you forth as lambs among wolves" (Luke 10:3). Isaiah, wishing to picture the new earth in extreme contrast with the present, said, "The wolf and the lamb shall feed together" (Isa. 65:25).

In Palestine the herdsmen do not drive the sheep, but rather lead them. The dog only protects them against enemies. The shepherd calls his flock, and they follow him. If he has a small flock, he names each member individually and they answer to their names. At night he leads them into stone-walled enclosures or caves called sheepfolds, where they will be safe.

Biologists believe that domestic sheep all descended from two wild species, the urial of Asia and the mouflon of southern Europe. From them came many varieties. By the time of Abraham herdsmen already recognized five different breeds.

The most common sheep in Palestine during the biblical period was the fat-tailed, also called the dumba. It was a tall, large-boned, long-nosed, round-backed animal with a black face and drooping ears. Such sheep stored fat in their rump and enormous tails, which often became so heavy that they dragged on the ground. To protect the tails the shepherds sometimes tied them to two-wheeled carts that carried them. A flock of fat-tailed sheep dragging the carts after them made quite a bit of noise, and the Talmud prohibited the owners from allowing the sheep to leave their fold on the Sabbath. Fortunately for the sheep, they did not all have tails that large. Today shepherds usually double back and tie the tails up to keep them off the ground. The fat in such a tail sometimes weighed 10 to 30 pounds and constituted about a fifth of the weight of the sheep. Exodus 29:22 refers to such fat-tailed sheep: "Thou shalt take of the ram the fat of the rump [margin: fat tail], and the fat that covereth the inwards." The rump fat caused the rounded back.

Mutton was a staple food among the Israelites. The choice meat was that of a yearling ram. The right shoulder they gave to the priest, the rest they boiled in water and allowed to cook thoroughly. Then they added milk, salt, and spices. After stripping the meat from the bones, they cracked the bones for their marrow. The broth they served with unleavened bread, which they dipped into the liquid and ate.

When the Israelites butchered rams, they heated the horns over a fire and straightened them to make into trumpets. They blew the trumpets at the Feast of Trumpets and other occasions. The seven priests, as you may recall, blew on trumpets of ram's horns as the Israelites marched around the city of Jericho.

At lambing time a ewe may have more than one offspring, but usually it will accept only one. In that case the shepherd tries to get another ewe that has lost a lamb to accept it. Failing in that, he may have to raise it himself, feeding it by hand. When there are more "bummer lambs" (as herders now call them) than he can take care of, he may give them to a poor family to raise. Usually tenderly cared for, they become household pets. It was such a one that the prophet Nathan referred to when he told David the story of the rich man who, when a traveler came to see him, took a poor man's ewe lamb for the feast instead of getting one from his own large flock (2 Sam. 12:4).

Ewes were valuable, not only for wool and for breeding purposes, but for the rich milk they supplied. The Hebrews kept it in goatskin bottles and made it into cheeses, much as they did with that of cows.

Wool was probably the most important product of sheep raising. In the semitropical climate of Palestine sheep did not grow heavy fleeces. They usually weighed only about three or four pounds as compared to the 20 to 30 pound fleeces now grown in more northern climates. The wool was shorn (probably with a sharp knife), washed, carded, and spun. In spinning, the Israelites did not use a spinning wheel, for it had not yet been invented. Instead they used a distaff and spindle. From the distaff, which held the wool under the left arm, they fed the fibers evenly by hand and twisted and wound them up on the spindle. The yarn they then wove on primitive looms into a heavy, warm cloth that they dyed and made into cloaks to wear by day and to sleep in at night.

The sheep-shearing time usually became something of a spring festival.

The men gathered together in a working bee during the day and often celebrated at night. Jacob chose the time when Laban was preoccupied with his sheep shearing to leave with his flock, wives, and children (Gen. 31:19-21). Judah, after the death of his wife (Gen. 38:12), went to his shearers, encountering his disguised daughter-in-law on the way. The sheep-shearing of Nabal (1 Sam. 25:4-12) and Absalom (2 Sam. 13:23, 24) were also at first festive occasions.

The fleeces of butchered sheep were often made into coats for shepherds and others who could not afford woven cloaks. We read in Hebrews 11:37, 38 of the "destitute, afflicted, tormented" saints who "wandered about in sheepskins and goatskins . . . (of whom the world was not worthy)." The skins of young lambs had the fleece removed. Stretched when wet, and then dried, the skins became the finest vellum, or parchment, on which the early scribes recorded the Scriptures.

The Bible says much about the lamb as a sacrifice. The lamb had to be without blemish of any kind, for it represented Christ, the Lamb of God, who would one day be sacrificed for the sins of the world. A lamb was slain at the Feast of the Passover. In this case the Israelite did not have it burnt on the altar. At the time of the Exodus from Egypt the head of the household sprinkled the blood on the doorposts to stay the hand of the angel of death. The family roasted the body of the lamb and had to eat it all or burn it before morning (Exodus 12).

SEA COW—see Dugong

SEA MONSTER—see Whale

SPECKLED BIRD—see Hyena

STAG—see Deer

SWINE; pig, hog (chazir) (choiros); *Sus scrofa. H 18"*

The KJV employs the words "swine" and "sow" for what we today call hog and pig. The Authorized Version uses "boar," but only in reference to the wild hog, not as we employ it today to denote the male. The female is, of course, still a sow, the young are piglets, or as a group they are a litter or raft.

For an animal domesticated as long as the hog, it does not receive much mention in the Bible. When it does, the reference is invariably derogatory. Several passages call attention to the Levitical prohibition against the eating of swine's flesh, and to the "abominable thing." Though Scripture lists several animals as unclean, the Hebrews seem to have a special abhorrence for swine that seems to antedate the Mosaic laws. They often appear to find it difficult even to use the word "swine" and would instead say, "that beast" or "the abomination."

The hog does have cloven hooves, but the dew claws at the back of the foot are so large and long that we can properly say that they have four hooves. The fact that it does not chew the cud kept it out of the class of clean animals contained in Leviticus 11 and Deuteronomy 14. Actually we know of no scientific basis for separating "clean" animals from "unclean" by either cloven hoofs or chewing the cud. Rather, it appears to be an arbitrary system that they could understand, and that probably had some good reason behind it at the time. Not only the Jews, but also the Moslem Arabs consider the swine as unfit for food.

The Jews felt so strongly about eating pork that during the time of the Maccabees, Eleazar, a 90-year-old man, refused to eat pork or even pretend to eat it. The soldiers of Antiochus IV (Epiphanes) pried Eleazar's mouth open and inserted pork, but he would not set a bad example to the younger ones. As a consequence, the soldiers put him to death. The Hellenistic authorities beat a mother and her seven sons because they would not eat pork. Then the king's men tortured, dismembered, and roasted the boys one after the other before her eyes. Yet she would not yield. She herself accepted torture and roasting rather than yield on the point.

The Greeks and Romans were fond of pork and raised large herds of swine. The herd that Jesus allowed the demons to enter when He cast them out of the demoniacs at Gadara was likely owned by Greeks who lived in the region around the Decapolis.

The Jews could think of no occupation so low and demeaning as that of a swineherd. The son or daughter of a swineherd was right at the bottom of the social castes and could not hope to marry anyone outside of his or her own profession. In the parable of the prodigal son Jesus showed the son's complete degradation by making him herd swine and want to eat the husks that they consumed.

In this connection it might be appropriate to mention that the husks the swine ate were not corncobs, as is so often pictured, but the pods of the carob or locust tree. Corn is an American cereal that was unknown in the Holy Land at the time. When the KJV uses the word "corn" it refers to wheat, barley, or millet.

Aside from being included in the Levitical injunction against eating pork, the swine does harbor a number of parasites that employ human beings as hosts during part of their life cycle. Important among them is the roundworm that causes trichinosis. It causes digestive problems, muscular pain, and inflammation. Pork must be either frozen or cooked thoroughly to kill the cysts embedded in the muscles. Smoked hams not cooked or frozen probably carry the greatest risk of trichina. As scavengers, pigs also pick up other diseases and transmit them. Some have thought that eating pork in hot climates was conducive to acquiring leprosy, but the Jews avoided pork and still had the disease among them in Bible times.

Many think of swine as dirty because they love to wallow in the mud. The problem is that they have no sweat glands and have to lie in the cool mud and water on hot days to get some relief. Peter loosely quotes from

Proverbs 26:11: "The dog is turned to his own vomit again; and the sow that was washed to her wallowing in the mire" (2 Peter 2:22). Other animals, such as the water buffalo, the rhinoceros, and the elephant, also like to lie in the mud. On today's farms hogs kept in sanitary conditions are as clean as any other livestock.

UNICORN (mistranslation of re'em). See also Aurochs.

"Will the unicorn be willing to serve thee, or abide by thy crib? Canst thou bind the unicorn with his band in the furrow? or will he harrow the valleys after thee?" (Job 39:9, 10).

Unfortunately, translators rendered the Hebrew word *re'em* as "unicorn" in the Septuagint and also in the KJV. The word appears nine times in the King James Version of the Scriptures. The unicorn is, of course, a legendary creature of Greek mythology. The creature was supposed to look like a horse with a single, spirally twisted horn coming out of its forehead. It appears on the British coat of arms opposite the rampant lion. C. S.

Lewis has given it publicity in some of his allegories, and so have many others. The legend may have grown from tales that travelers told of the Indian rhinoceros. The rhino does not look at all like the unicorn of legend, any more than does the manatee resemble a mermaid.

An examination of some of the texts that mention *re'em* tends to point to an altogether different animal. Job 39:9-12 depicts a powerful draft animal, yet too wild to manage. It parallels the work of an ox, but is bigger and more unmanageable. Balaam's prophecies about Israel in Numbers 23:22 and 24:8 describe the nation as having the strength of a unicorn. In Deuteronomy 33:17 Moses, in blessing Israel, portrays it as having the glory of a firstborn bullock, "and his horns are like the horns of unicorns [wild ox, margin); with them he shall push the people together to the ends of the earth." The phrasing suggests that it had two horns rather than one, and also that they pointed forward. Other translations have "wild ox" instead of unicorn. David speaks in Psalm 29:6 of the cedars of Lebanon skipping "like a calf; Lebanon and Sirion like a young unicorn." The parallelism indicates the similarity between the young calf and the young unicorn.

Psalm 92:10 declares that the righteous shall be exalted "like the horn of an unicorn." The verse seems to indicate a singular horn, but the marginal reference indicates that it is the trumpeting horn that the psalmist refers to. It is quite possible that the Israelites made the horns of the *re'em* into trumpets and used them to praise the Lord.

The relief on the Ishtar Gate, called the Unicorn of Babylon, is actually an aurochs. The profile view makes the two horns appear to be one and has given excuse for the misnomer.

With all this in mind, please turn to the entry under aurochs and see if this is not the powerful, oxlike animal with the forward pointing horns that could fulfill all the requirements of *re'em* when rightly understood.

VOLE—see Mouse

WEASEL (choled); *Erminia erminia*. L 10″
FERRET; *Mustela putorius*.
MONGOOSE; *Herpestes nyula*.

The term weasel appears only once in the Bible (Lev. 11:29), along with other animals pronounced as unclean to the Hebrews. It is not at all certain that the weasel is the animal intended by the biblical writer. *The New English Bible* translates the Hebrew as "mole-rat," and that may be nearer to the truth. There are, however, weasels in Palestine, as well as a number of their relatives such as the polecats, and mongooses. People may have grouped all of them together under one name in Bible times.

The weasel is small, lithe, and extremely active. Knowing no fear, it appears as willing to attack a man as a mouse. Its food consists largely of mice, rats, other small rodents, bird eggs, and young birds. Because of its small head and slim body, it can follow rodents down into their burrows and catch them. Also, it can climb trees and run down squirrels along the branches.

Weasels are a rich brown above and white below, with a black tail tip. During winter, in northern climates, it changes its fur color to white, and

91

is known as an ermine. The tail tip remains black. Its fur was greatly prized and used as trim on royal coronation robes.

The name ferret, also listed with the unclean animals, refers to the polecat, a larger relative of the weasel. In this case the translation should probably have been "gecko," a small lizard, rather than ferret. It is so translated in more recent translations.

The Egyptian mongoose, also found in Palestine, was probably thought of as a larger weasel, though the Scriptures do not specifically refer to it. Its lithe body and lightning-like movements are weasel-like.

WHALE, SPERM (tannim) (ketos); *Physeter catadon.* L 55'

The whale has been the subject of considerable misunderstanding, especially among amateur Bible students. In the forefront of the controversy is the story of Jonah. Could a whale swallow the prophet? Could he remain alive for three days in the belly of a whale?

Biologists point to the fact that the throats of most whales are large enough to swallow only the small fish and krill that they feed on—in spite of the fact that a whale may weigh as much as 30 elephants. It is true, however, that the sperm whale, which lives in all warm oceans, has different dietary habits and can swallow seals and dolphins. Records claim that whales have swallowed men a number of times. No reliable account exists, though, of men who remained alive in them for three days.

James Bradley, a whaler on the *Star of the East*, was reportedly swallowed by a sperm whale in "southern waters" in 1891. The next morning when the men cut open the captured whale they found him inside, unconscious but alive. After four weeks he recovered sufficiently to tell about his experience. Robert Cushman Murphy, a world authority on whales, debunked the story in an article in the April 1947 *Natural History* magazine.

He says that a man swallowed by a whale would stay alive just about as long as if someone had held him under water. He cites a number of cliches in the story that appear to give authenticity, but actually supply no proof. The account offers no definite source. The author was "browsing through some old records." He found "well authenticated facts," but gives no proof. "The heat of the whale drained all the strength from the man's body." Actually the body temperature of a whale is about one degree higher than that of man. The whale's stomach acids caused his skin to be "bleached white as snow." That just does not happen to a whale's meal. The ship *Star of the East* is not on the list of American whaling ships, and Murphy doubts whether it is on the British or any other.

Another account tells of Sayita, a fisherman on the coast of Lagos, Africa, who jumped from shore into the mouth of a whale he had harpooned. The whale swallowed him, but he lived to tell about it. His friends pulled the whale ashore, opened it up, and found Sayita inside. This sounds just about as "fishy" as the previous story.

In the June 1947 issue of *Natural History* magazine, in the letter section, appears a firsthand account by a young ship's doctor on a sealing ship in the year 1893 or 1894, who opened up a whale after it had swallowed a man. He found the sealer not only severely lacerated and badly crushed, but also covered with digestive juices and heavy slime. The odor was so strong and the appearance of the partly digested man so revolting that they were relieved to be able to consign him to the sea.

All the contention about the whale and Jonah is really beside the point in a way, because the book of Jonah does not even mention a whale. Jonah 1:17 clearly states, "Now the Lord had prepared a great fish to swallow up Jonah." Just what the fish was is not certain. It may have been a shark, or a fish especially prepared for the occasion, as stated. Matthew 12:40, where Christ refers to Jonah's being three days in "the whale's belly" uses the Greek word *keta*. It should have been translated *sea monster*.

The whale is not a fish, but a warm-blooded mammal that bears its young alive and suckles them. Like other mammals, it has to hold its breath under water and blow out the spent air when it comes to the surface. That is when the whalers holler, "Thar she blows!" They can distinguish the different species of whales by the shape of the spray. It is not a geyser of water, but mostly warm air and condensing moisture.

Genesis 1:21 mentions God as creating whales on the fifth day together with the fish and birds. God made the mammals a day later. That seems inconsistent, and it is. The Hebrew *tannim,* translated "whale" in a number of places in the KJV, should read "sea monsters." Most modern translations do render it that way. It is a general term and could mean whales or large fish or reptiles. The fossil records tell us that a large number of gigantic fish and reptiles lived in the sea during prehistoric times, and the "sea monsters" may have originally been references to them.

We are still left with the problem of how Jonah lived for three days in the belly of a sea monster, and we will not try to explain it by natural means. In this case the Lord performed a miracle to suit His inscrutable purposes. We may as well leave it at that.

WISENT—see Aurochs

WOLF, SYRIAN (zeeb, lukos); *Canis lupis syriacus.* L 54"

The Syrian wolf is a variety of the European species that ranges over most of the Northern Hemisphere. A little smaller in size, in color it tends to be more brownish and lighter. Its fur is not as heavy as that of the more northern animals. In Bible times it was a fairly common wild animal in Palestine, and most people knew of it even if they had not seen it. Today it appears only rarely in the Transjordan region, the extreme southern part of the range of wolves.

Despite the fact that it was well-known, we do not find one incident regarding it in Scripture. Instead, the Bible always speaks of it in symbolic terms or in prophecy. Consider the following examples: "her judges are evening wolves" (Zeph. 3:3); "her princes in the midst thereof are like wolves" (Eze. 22:27); "I send you forth as lambs among wolves" (Luke 10:3); and "false prophets, which come to you in sheep's clothing, but inwardly they are ravening wolves" (Matt. 7:15). In all instances but one in the Bible the wolf represents evil men. The one exception is Genesis 49:27, where Jacob blesses his 12 sons, and Benjamin is said to "ravin as a wolf." It is not exactly a compliment, or a blessing, either. Benjamin was noted for his warlike nature.

The Bible often uses the terms *ravin* and *ravenous* in connection with the wolf. They refer to the fact that it is a predator, grabbing and eating its prey. Man has a tendency to fear the unknown and to build up legends about night animals and birds, such as bats, owls, and wolves, about which he knows little. He has made up stories about werewolves (people who take on the form of wolves at night) and other alleged supernatural activities of wolves. We like also to repeat stories of packs of wolves that kept villages in fear and that followed sleighs and killed the occupants. Some of the stories have their basis in things that actually happened many years ago. Bible writers were no doubt familiar with similar stories that may have colored some of their statements about wolves. To them, wolves were fierce, bloodthirsty predators, out to kill and destroy.

They had some reason for such an attitude, because sheep grazing on the open hillsides appeared to wolves to be legitimate prey. The pastoralists of Bible times learned to look upon the wolf as a raider of sheep, against whom they must constantly remain on guard. Sheep are stupid and will bunch together when attacked, giving wolves opportunity to kill more than they need or can eat.

Another term used in connection with wolves in the Bible is *evening*. The Septuagint translates it as "of Arabia" because the Hebrew term for evening can also mean Arabia. Some translators believe it should be "desert" or "plain," as rendered in *The New English Bible*. It is hard to know what the original writers had in mind, but in this case it probably does not matter very much. Evening is the time when wolves come out to hunt after remaining hidden in rocky caves during the day.

Recent studies of wolves have shown that folklore has greatly maligned the character of the animals. For one thing, they have found that not one incident of wolves attacking people in the past 100 years can be substantiated. The wolves themselves are on the whole kindly animals, not fighting among themselves, but sharing in the work of feeding and looking after the young belonging to a fellow member of their group. When a biologist entered a wild wolf den in Alaska and handled the cubs, the adults stood nervously by, anxious about their offspring, but they did not attack.

They kill game animals for food, but usually weed out the sick or maimed that cannot keep up with the herd. In this way they improve the quality of the breeding stock. Man goes about killing the best and biggest in the herd to collect as trophies. He usually does not need the food.

In Palestine, wolves usually hunted singly or in small family groups. They did not band together in large packs as they apparently did on the Russian steppes in winter. For this reason the country people did not think of them as man-killers. They were just predators of their flocks. That is what Paul had in mind when he spoke in Acts 20:29 of "grievous wolves" (false teachers) who would follow him, enter his churches, "not sparing the flock," and mislead many of his members.